"It is fitting that I write these w... in October... ...Memo-
rial of Pope St. John Paul II, w... canon... ...ril 11,
2000, the first canonization of ...new ... ...ly on
that occasion, the Holy Father ...ad, 'In ... ...en the... ...
and Second World Wars that Cl... ...entrusted h... ...message of mercy to
her. Those who remember, who were witnesses and participants in the
events of those years and the horrible sufferings they caused for millions
of people, know well how necessary was the message of mercy.' In the
face of our current suffering in the world today, Susan Tassone had made
the message of mercy wonderfully accessible in a beautiful way in her
book *Praying with Jesus and Faustina during Lent and in Times of Suffering.* Joining our prayers with Jesus and St. Faustina throughout the days
of Lent will help God's suffering children to come to the experience of
His Divine Mercy."

—Most Reverend Thomas John Paprocki,
    Bishop of Springfield in Illinois

"Suffering and sorrow uniquely mark every day and time as well as the
people who occupy it. And so, too, this moment, and each of us in it.
How precious, then, is this beautiful book of meditations. When problems
persist and doubt disturbs, turn to this treasury of grace and drink deeply
of the wisdom offered to us through St. Faustina and other mystic saints.
Hope will not hesitate, peace will be restored, and joy will be found.
Thank you, Susan Tassone!"

—Johnnette Benkovic Williams, Host, EWTN Television and Radio
    Founder, Women of Grace®

"This is a phenomenal gem helping us to discover the heart of St. Faustina's spirituality and to understand her insights on the value of suffering when united to the Passion of Christ. The meditations on the Passion taken from St. Faustina's *Diary* are a huge aid to any person's prayer life."

> — FATHER DAN CAMBRA, M.I.C., Holy Souls Sodality of The National Shrine of The Divine Mercy

"Susan Tassone's new book reads like a timeless classic that should be in the hands of every Catholic! Today, when there is confusion about the meaning and value of human suffering, this book radiates the splendor of truth for growth in prayer and virtue. Susan skillfully organizes St. Faustina's masterpiece, the *Diary*, into relevant pearls of wisdom together with her own insights, leading readers to discover anew Christ's merciful love. This work will enhance your Lenten journey by drawing you into divine intimacy. In times of suffering, you'll reach for this book to find heavenly wisdom and strength. The Eucharist, the Virgin Mary, and priesthood are beautifully featured also. Highly recommended!"

> — KATHLEEN BECKMAN, Author, *A Family Guide to Spiritual Warfare* and *Praying for Priests*

"Susan Tassone has offered us an ability to grow in our relationship with Our Lord through the insights of St. Faustina and prayerful devotions. I urge Catholics to use this work for a spiritually profitable Lenten experience."

> — MOST REVEREND JEROME E. LISTECKI, Archbishop of Milwaukee

"In her latest book, *Praying with Jesus and Faustina during Lent and in Times of Suffering,* Susan Tassone continues to walk in the footsteps of St. Faustina Kowalska by being one of the most ardent apostles of the Divine Mercy. Did not Our Lord say to St. Faustina that her suffering will be a sign that He was with her? It's for each of us. Let this book be a guide for you to draw closer to Jesus especially during those challenging and grievous times we must all undergo to gain eternal life. Jesus, I Trust in You!"

— MOTHER MARIE ANDRÉ, P.C.P.A., Abbess of Our Lady of Solitude Monastery, Phoenix, Arizona

"Susan Tassone's book *Praying with Jesus and Faustina during Lent and in Times of Suffering* reveals the Christian truth that suffering is salvific — it has a saving aspect and is not to be wasted. When united to the Cross of Jesus Christ, suffering takes on new meaning. The communication and dialogue between Jesus and St. Faustina that Tassone sets forth profoundly illustrates this reality. This book is a wonderful, spiritual read, especially during the liturgical season of Lent and in times of personal suffering."

— FR. WADE MENEZES, C.P.M., Fathers of Mercy Assistant General and EWTN Series and Radio Host

"As a Passionist priest, I know Jesus' sufferings have great merit. St. Paul of the Cross said, 'Meditation on the Passion of Jesus is the shortest way to holiness.' Many saints, such as St. Faustina, have proclaimed this truth. Her meditations on the Passion of Christ will help unite you to Jesus. I highly recommend this book for anyone seeking a closer walk with Jesus especially in times of suffering."

— FR. CEDRIC PISEGNA, C.P. , Creator, *Live with Passion!*

PRAYING WITH JESUS AND FAUSTINA
DURING LENT
AND IN TIMES OF SUFFERING

PRAYING

WITH

JESUS

AND

FAUSTINA

during Lent and in Times of Suffering

SUSAN TASSONE

SOPHIA INSTITUTE PRESS
Manchester, New Hampshire

Sophia Institute Press
Box 5284, Manchester, NH 03108
1-800-888-9344
www.SophiaInstitute.com
Sophia Institute Press® is a registered trademark of Sophia Institute.

paperback ISBN 978-1-64413-427-6
ebook ISBN 978-1-64413-428-3
Library of Congress Control Number: 2020949656

First printing

To dear Father Dan Cambra, M.I.C.,
who was there from the start
and with me all the way.

CONTENTS

APPENDICES

FOREWORD

PARTICIPATING IN THE SACRIFICE OF THE CROSS

Bishop Joseph N. Perry
Auxiliary Bishop, Archdiocese of Chicago

In the *Liturgy of the Hours*, which bishops, priests, deacons, and religious are obliged to pray every day for the welfare of the Church and the Christian people, are found a few lines taken from the book of Job, chapter one. Reading the following passage, found in Wednesday's Morning Prayer of the Third Week in Ordinary Time, causes one to stop in one's tracks:

> Naked I came forth from my mother's womb, and naked I shall go back again. The Lord gave and the Lord has taken away; blessed be the name of the Lord! We accept good things from God; and should we not accept evil?

Should we not accept evil? These are troublesome words.

In evil's wake is often found suffering. Suffering as part of the human condition is one way to acquire holiness of life. Most Christians struggle with this prospect. The closer we approach an authentic relationship with Christ, the more we encounter manifestations of trouble and hardship. Why is this so? For reasons we cannot grasp, till perhaps in the Beatific Vision, God requires agony and suffering as a means for our reconciliation with Him, principally through the salvific act on the Cross of His most beloved Son, Jesus Christ.

Some of us will discover this saving way through sickness and physical pain, others by way of mental anguish, emotional upset, loss of loved ones, loss of fortune or the stability associated with employment or material gain, the daily variety of hardships and failures, the irritations suffered in our encounters with others. With these experiences and other akin to them, we are tempted to think we have lost our union with God or that God has abandoned us.

Christian faith teaches us that there is a dignity to be derived from suffering—if only because God chose human suffering as the instrument of our redemption. We live in a world that is convinced that suffering is inconvenient and must be avoided at all costs. But for all our wealth and good times, opportunities and choices, our lives are interrupted by reports of the agonies of countless people here and around the world, to say nothing of those of our relatives, loved ones, and friends. We are genuinely moved to our depths by witnessing or hearing about what people are asked to endure in their lives.

Our own lives are interrupted by anxiety, hurt, and misfortune. When someone asks us how we are doing, we give the knee-jerk response, "Oh, I'm fine!," when truthfully we are not fine. We are dealing with suffering in various times and in various ways and are embarrassed to mention that something might be less than fine.

But the Catholic Faith teaches us something different and refreshing. Catholic teaching on suffering has its origin in the lived example of Jesus Christ. Christ did not gloss over the reality of suffering. He worked with it and showed that all suffering of whatever sort when united to His sufferings can lead to sharing in His Resurrection.

St. Faustina Kowalska, whose reflections on the Passion and suffering you are about to read, said:

> If the angels were capable of envy they would envy us humans for two things: one is the privilege to receive Holy Communion; and the other is, suffering. (1804)

We already know the joy of receiving the Body and Blood of the Lord commingling with our human substance. But why would the angels be jealous of human suffering? The suffering of a Christian is a paradoxical conduit for intimacy with Jesus Christ. Suffering defined the life and ministry of Jesus. We are called to life in Christ no matter what happens on our earthly pilgrimage. With our desire to be close to Christ and to have Christ close to us, our sufferings make it possible for us to exist in solidarity with Him.

Christian life is one long effort to get next to Christ. Jesus bore our sins in His body as He hung upon the Cross. This is our inspiration. It is through our suffering in its various manifestations that we come to know the person of Jesus Christ and companion ourselves with Him through His most loving act on our behalf. If we deny the suffering Jesus, we deny God. As painful as suffering is, if it must come to us, it is a unique opportunity that we possess only in this life.

Saints and mystics tell us, as St. Faustina does in these pages, that if we embrace opportunities for suffering, whether small or great, we will not regret it in the life to come. This is our consolation up front in this life.

Suffering stretches us. It pushes us toward others. It encourages us to pray. It invites us to rely on a number of resources, particularly those from within. We develop character while we handle painful times.

Pain is a source of wisdom. It prepares us to help others whose experiences echo ours. Pain shared offers stories that help others who are lost and need our guidance.

When we reflect on our past, we can recall the pain we felt last month or last year: the pain of a lost love or the anxiety associated with losing a job and facing many bills in the wake, perhaps the pain of the death of a child or the pain of children launching out away from home or the death of a spouse or a dear friend. It might have seemed to us that we wouldn't be able to cope. But we did somehow. Coping strengthened us, especially with the power of prayer that held us up.

What we forget even now is that we need never experience a painful time alone. The agony that accompanies a wrenching situation is dissipated as quickly and as silently as the entrance of the higher power — our God when called upon.

We long for contentment, and we deserve such times. But somehow without the interruption brought by life's pain, we would fail to recognize the value of contentment.

God is the Holy One par excellence. We become holy by virtue of our relationship with God. All holiness is a reflection and extension of God's holiness. We can become holy when we try to remain faithful in the face of the suffering that may come into our lives.

We live in a broken world. And our individual lives are microcosms of this brokenness. Having walked this earthly path, Jesus promises that if we carry our crosses, He will meet us on the other side at Easter.

Here is a prayer from an Orthodox church prayer book:

The dark clouds of trouble gather above us, O Lord, and the grief of torments terrify us. Though we find ourselves in a state of suffering we do not complain against you, O Good One, for you are our support and the unshaken rock upon which we place our hope.

You know, O God, the cause of our wretchedness and sorrow, and you continue to look after us. Even in our suffering we know that you love us, and it is this very knowledge that strengthens us. Thus, hoping in your love and goodness we shall not allow these assaults to overcome us; rather we will fight with courage and confident in your help we shall be victorious.

It is you who guides the world and the fate of mortals; thus direct the ship of our lives which is assailed by the waves of temptation, so that it may reach the calm harbor. Alone we fight in vain against the tempests of life, for without you we can do nothing. We therefore fly to you, O Good One, and we pray: come to our aid and save us by your might, just as you once saved Peter, who came to you on the water. Stretch out your hand to us as you did to him, O Lord of mercy, and do not delay. Amen.

St. Paul reminds us in his letter to the Romans (8:5–27) that we are the children of God *and therefore are heirs as well—heirs of God, heirs with Christ if only we suffer with Him so as to be glorified with Him.* St. Paul says further, "I consider the sufferings of the present to be as nothing compared with the glory to be revealed in us."

In the words of Cardinal Robert Sarah, Prefect of the Vatican Congregation for Divine Worship and the Discipline of the Sacraments:

We cannot live as Christians without participating in the Sacrifice of the Cross in which the Lord Jesus gives himself unreservedly to save, by his death, humanity which had died because of sin. The Redeemer associates humanity with himself and leads it back to the Father. In the embrace of the Crucified One all human suffering finds light and comfort.[1]

Interestingly enough, when Jesus rose from the dead with a glorified body, notice that He kept His wounds: the marks of pain and suffering did not disappear. When we rise to meet Him at the end, our glorified bodies

---

[1] Robert Cardinal Sarah, letter to bishops around the world (August 15, 2020).

may be allowed to bear marks that serve as reminders of the suffering we endured in life. The season of Lent followed by Holy Week and Easter affords us the opportunity to contemplate the mystery of the risen Jesus and His glorified wounds, with hope!

So, believers that we are, let us walk with Christ, who has taken upon Himself our sufferings and carried our sorrows to lead us by means of His cross to the joy of the Resurrection.

PREFACE

JESUS, ST. FAUSTINA, SUFFERING ... AND US

Let me tell you my "St. Faustina story." I'm sure all of us who have a devotion to her—are fans of hers—have one.

I "met" this amazing mystic in the 1980s ... on my lunch break. I had walked over to Chicago's St. Peter's Church in the Loop for Mass and then popped into the church's gift shop to do a bit of browsing.

And there I stumbled upon a diary. Her diary. *The* diary.

Now, I've loved reading published diaries ever since I was a young girl, starting with Anne Frank's. Flipping through the pages of St. Faustina's, I came across the Divine Mercy Chaplet ... and I was hooked. I felt an immediate connection with this nun who had died—at that time—half a century earlier.

She wasn't an unknown then but was a "not-well-known" outside her native Poland. Not yet even declared Venerable.

I bought the book, took it home after work, and immediately began praying the chaplet daily, especially for those who were dying. I highlighted passages I loved, ones that really hit home for me. (I used a *lot* of highlighter ink.) And I even marched in a Columbus Day parade raising her banner high!

Over and over that first year, I prayed, "Jesus, I trust in You." But did I? I wanted to, but I wasn't sure if I did. Now, looking back, after having nine books on the holy souls in purgatory published, I *am* sure Jesus trusted in me — me, who became "the Purgatory Lady," who has twice had the privilege of meeting St. John Paul II because of my work on purgatory.

Flash-forward more than two decades, when I found myself sitting in the dignitary section high above St. Peter's Square on April 30, 2000, peering down at the Polish pontiff who was canonizing his beloved Sister Faustina of the Blessed Sacrament.

My beloved.

Your beloved.

The world's beloved.

Thousands upon thousands upon thousands packed the square and heard the pope tell us in his homily:

Today my joy is truly great in presenting the life and witness of Sister Faustina Kowalska to the whole Church as a gift of God for our time. By Divine Providence, the life of this humble daughter of

Poland was completely linked with the history of the 20th century, the century we have just left behind. In fact, it was between the First and Second World Wars that Christ entrusted his message of mercy to her. Those who remember, who were witnesses and participants in the events of those years and the horrible sufferings they caused for millions of people, know well how necessary was the message of mercy.

Jesus told Sister Faustina: "Humanity will not find peace until it turns trustfully to divine mercy." Through the work of the Polish religious, this message has become linked forever to the 20th century, the last of the second millennium and the bridge to the third. It is not a new message but can be considered a gift of special enlightenment that helps us to relive the Gospel of Easter more intensely, to offer it as a ray of light to the men and women of our time.

What will the years ahead bring us? What will man's future on earth be like? We are not given to know. However, it is certain that in addition to new progress there will unfortunately be no lack of painful experiences. But the light of divine mercy, which the Lord in a way wished to return to the world through Sister Faustina's charism, will illumine the way for the men and women of the third millennium.

A new millennium, a new century, and its second decade unfolded. On an October weekend in 2014, I visited the National Shrine of the Divine

Mercy in Stockbridge, Massachusetts. There I met Father Dan Cambra, M.I.C., a purgatory "fan" who asked me if I would ever consider writing a book (the first!) about St. Faustina's devotion to the holy souls.

Oh, yes!

I wrote that and had it published, and then Father Dan had a suggestion for another, and another, and another, and another, and finally for this one: *Praying with Jesus and Faustina during Lent and in Times of Suffering*.

Six years, six books. A lot of time — wonderful times — studying, praying, and reading and rereading the *Diary*. I found, and shared, something new with each book.

I have had the joy and privilege of introducing many readers to St. Faustina and of deepening a relationship and understanding for others who already knew her.

So, why a book on Lent and suffering? Throughout the *Diary*, Jesus asks St. Faustina (and us) to meditate on His Passion and His great love for us: why God made us, why Jesus suffered and died for us. For all of us but for each of us. For me. For you.

My prayer, my hope, my goal with this book is that it will help you learn to more deeply:

- Meditate with Jesus and St. Faustina daily during Lent and in times of suffering
- Participate in St. Faustina's vision of Christ's Passion
- Find comfort and strength from the crucified Christ

- Pray the Stations of the Cross using the words of Jesus and St. Faustina

- Join your sufferings to Christ's sorrowful Passion

- Find refuge, consolation, and mercy in Christ's wounds

- Unite your sorrows with the sufferings that afflicted Our Lady's heart

- Get a "firsthand look" at purgatory

- Pray a variety of litanies for the troubled times of your life

- Come to appreciate the beauty and value of Confession, from the words of Jesus and St. Faustina

And please know and remember this:

In times of personal, public, or even pandemic suffering, Jesus and His beloved St. Faustina are always with us. They're always with you.

You remain in my prayers.

> —Susan
> Feast of St. Faustina
> October 5, 2020

Acknowledgments

To my superheroes,
    Steve Gross,
    Bert Ghezzi,
    Bill Dodds, and
    Jackie Lindsey,
whose talents, professionalism, and friendship made all the difference.

    And to my dear ones: my three nephews and niece—Steven, Bruce, Mark, and Kristine—their mother, Rusty, and Adam.

    Thanks for cheering me on!

INTRODUCTION

LIVING THROUGH A TIME OF DARKNESS

Father Joseph Roesch, M.I.C.
Vicar General, Rome

The publication of this new book by Susan Tassone could not be more timely in this era of suffering that the world has been enduring because of COVID-19 and the unrest, violence, and divisions that have marked the recent past. Pope Francis has said more than once that it is as if a new world war has already begun in a piecemeal way. At times during the past year in our country, it has seemed as if a new civil war has begun.

In the midst of all this, Susan gives us a beautiful treasure in *Praying with Jesus and Faustina during Lent and in Times of Suffering*. In this work, she has created another powerful spiritual handbook that is very practical yet extremely profound. Once again, we drink deeply from the spiritual riches that can be found in *Divine Mercy in My Soul*, the *Diary* of St. Faustina. But we also come to know other holy saints and mystics who teach us important lessons on suffering, faith, and some beautiful spiritual practices. The prayers and reflections found here help us to enter into the holiest time of the Church's liturgical year, Lent and Easter. Jesus and St. Faustina teach us how to use fruitfully the season of Lent as a preparation for the joy of Easter. By reflecting on Christ's Paschal Mystery, we can come to understand the mystery of suffering in the world and the role that suffering plays in our lives.

"And the Word became flesh and dwelt among us" (John 1:14). The second Person of the Holy Trinity became Jesus Christ, a man like us in all things but sin. He came to show us how to live and how to die. He came to reveal the merciful face of His Father and to reveal to us our ultimate destiny, the glory that God has prepared for each of us. Susan has astutely chosen some beautiful passages from the *Diary* of St. Faustina to teach us these mysteries. By meditating on Christ's Passion with St. Faustina, we come to understand our calling to take up the cross.

Good Friday is not the end of the story, and it does not last forever. Easter Sunday will come for each of us, and the Paschal joy of heaven is something that will never end! St. Faustina came to understand the Paschal Mystery intimately. She lived on this earth for thirty-three years, just as Jesus did, and she suffered a great deal during her life. Her sufferings came in many forms — physical sufferings, misunderstandings, doubts, humiliations, and mistreatments. Jesus was her teacher in the spiritual life. He once asked her to share even her misery with Him (see *Diary*, 1318).

When St. Faustina was a young girl, she had to leave school after a few years to help her family on their farm. Despite her meager education, her *Diary*, which was inspired by her mystical experiences, is an extremely rich resource in which we can learn about the spiritual life. In fact, many people are calling for St. Faustina to be declared a Doctor of the Church. She meets the criteria: she lived a life of extraordinary holiness, her writings have made a significant contribution to the authentic Catholic tradition, and they exhibit a depth of doctrinal understanding and fresh insight into the mysteries of the Faith. Her message has current and lasting value, she bore witness to her Faith in her life, and she has inspired many by her spiritual and mystical witness. Let us pray that she may be declared a Doctor of the Church.

Our world has been living through a time of darkness. But by praying with Jesus, Mary, St. Faustina, and the other saints in this beautiful book, we can find the light and hope of Christ. In her book, Susan leads us to discover the beauty of the sacrament of Confession, which unfortunately is neglected by many. The passages from the *Diary* of St. Faustina that Susan has chosen are extremely helpful in helping us to prepare to make a good confession and to avoid the temptations and assaults of the evil one. Susan also helps us to learn about the spiritual practice of fasting, which Jesus highly recommended to overcome evil. There are also many prayers and litanies that are also powerful remedies against the evil in the world.

We are never alone. Jesus is always with us. He wouldn't leave us as spiritual orphans in our time of need. I am certain that you will profit spiritually from this gem that Susan has created just when we need it!

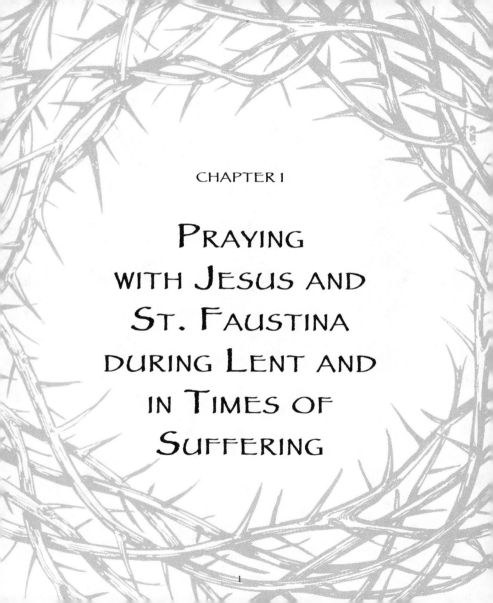

CHAPTER 1

PRAYING WITH JESUS AND ST. FAUSTINA DURING LENT AND IN TIMES OF SUFFERING

SHROVE TUESDAY

FAUSTINA: One day, I saw two roads. One was broad, covered with ... flowers, full of joy, music and all sorts of pleasures. People ... reached the end without realizing it. And at the end ... was a horrible precipice; that is, the abyss of hell. The souls fell blindly into it; as they walked, so they fell.... And I saw the other road, or rather, a path, for it was narrow and strewn with thorns and rocks; and the people who walked along it had tears in their eyes, and all kinds of suffering befell them.... At the end of the road there was a magnificent garden filled with all sorts of happiness, and all these souls entered there. At the very first instant they forgot all their sufferings. (153)

JESUS: **You please me most when you meditate on My Sorrowful Passion. Join your little sufferings to My Sorrowful Passion, so that they may have infinite value before My Majesty.** (1512)

FAUSTINA: ... I meditated on Jesus' terrible Passion, and I understood that what I was suffering was nothing compared to the Savior's Passion, and that even the smallest imperfection was the cause of this terrible suffering. Then my soul was filled with very great contrition, and only then I sensed that I was in the sea of the unfathomable mercy of God. (654)

My Jesus, let my sacrifice burn before Your throne in all silence, but with the full force of love, as I beg You to have mercy on souls. (1342)

PRAYER

Dear Lord, give me strength to bear my crosses and to offer my sufferings in union with You and Your Mother, Our Lady of Sorrows.

IN TIMES OF SUFFERING

Lead me, O God, along whatever roads you please; I have placed all my trust in Your will, which is for me love and mercy itself. (1264)

Grant that I may love You, O Jesus, and that I may love You
in my family life,
in the exact fulfillment of my daily duties,
and in the acceptance of those crosses connected with
my state in life.

Grant that I may love You, O Jesus, in the souls whom You have
committed to my care,
especially those who have gone astray.

Grant that I may love You, O Jesus, in Your ineffable gift of the
heart of Mary,
that I may learn to be simple, humble, chaste, and pure,
and that guided by Mary, I may sanctify myself in Your love.

You know that in spite of my miseries, I desire with a resolute will
to live and to die saying and proving to You
that I love You above all treasures of heaven and earth.

ASH WEDNESDAY

FAUSTINA: Today is Ash Wednesday. During Holy Mass, I felt for a short time the Passion of Jesus in my members. Lent is a very special time for the work of priests. We should assist them in rescuing souls. (931)

At the same time, I saw a certain person [Father Sopocko] and, in part, the condition of his soul and the ordeals God was sending him. His sufferings were of the mind and in a form so acute that I pitied him and said to the Lord, "Why do you treat him like that?" (604)

JESUS: **For the sake of his triple crown (604) ... that of virginity, the priesthood and martyrdom (596) ... I permit these adversities in order to increase his merit. I do not reward for good results but for the patience and hardship undergone for My sake.** (86)

PRAYER FOR THE HOLY CHURCH AND PRIESTS

O my Jesus, I beg You ... [to] give power to the words of priests so that hardened hearts might be brought to repentance and return to You, O Lord. Lord, give us holy priests; You yourself maintain them in holiness. O Divine and Great High Priest, may the power of Your mercy accompany them everywhere and protect them from the devil's traps and snares which are continually being set for the souls of priests. May the power of Your mercy, O Lord, shatter and bring to naught all that might tarnish the sanctity of priests, for You can do all things. (1052)

Dear Lord, I pray for priests especially N., N., and N.

PRAYER

Dear Lord, give me strength to bear my crosses and to offer my sufferings in union with You and Your Mother, Our Lady of Sorrows.

IN TIMES OF SUFFERING

And the Lord also gave me to understand what unimaginable glory awaits the person who resembles the suffering Jesus here on earth. That person will resemble Jesus in His glory. (604)

Today I place my heart on the paten where Your Heart has been placed, O Jesus, and today I offer myself together with You to God, Your Father and mine, as a sacrifice of love and praise. Father of Mercy, look upon the sacrifice of my heart, but through the wound in the Heart of Jesus. (239)

THURSDAY AFTER ASH WEDNESDAY

FAUSTINA: Small practices for Lent. Although I wish and desire to do so, I cannot practice big mortifications as before, because I am under the strict surveillance of the doctor. But I can practice little things: first—sleep without a pillow; keep myself a little hungry; every day, with my arms outstretched, say the chaplet which the Lord taught me; occasionally, with arms outstretched, for an indefinite period of time pray informally. Intention: to beg divine mercy for poor sinners, and for priests, the power to bring sinful hearts to repentance. (934)

JESUS: **I have need of your sufferings to rescue souls** (1612). **There is but one price at which souls are bought, and that is suffering united to My suffering on the cross** (324). **You will join prayers, fasts, mortifications, labors and all sufferings to My prayer, fasting, mortifications, labors and sufferings and then they will have power before My Father.** (531)

PRAYER

O Savior of the world, I unite myself with Your mercy. My Jesus, I join all my sufferings to Yours and deposit them in the treasury of the Church for the benefit of souls. (740)

Dear Lord, give me strength to bear my crosses and to offer my sufferings in union with You and Your Mother, Our Lady of Sorrows.

IN TIMES OF SUFFERING

True love is measured by the thermometer of suffering. (343) O my Jesus, my soul was yearning for the days of trial, but do not leave me alone in the darkness of my soul. Rather, do You hold me firmly, close to Yourself. Set a guard over my lips, so that the fragrance of my sufferings may be known and pleasing to You alone. (831)

FRIDAY AFTER ASH WEDNESDAY

FAUSTINA: At the beginning of Lent, I also asked to have the subject of my particular examen changed, and I was told to do everything with the pure intention of reparation for poor sinners. This keeps me in continual union with God, and this intention perfects my actions, because everything I do is done for immortal souls. All hardships and fatigue are as nothing when I think that they reconcile sinful souls with God. (619)

JESUS: **Tell souls where they are to look for solace; that is, in the Tribunal of Mercy [the Sacrament of Reconciliation]. There the greatest miracles take place [and] are incessantly repeated (1448). Here the misery of the soul meets the God of mercy. Tell souls that from this fount of mercy souls draw graces solely with the vessel of trust. If their trust is great, there is no limit to My generosity. The torrents of grace inundate humble souls. The proud remain always in poverty and misery, because My grace turns away from them to humble souls.** (1602)

PRAYER

For quite a long while, I felt pain in my hands, feet, and side. Then I saw a certain sinner who, profiting from my sufferings, drew near to the Lord. All this for starving souls that they may not die of starvation. (1468)

Dear Lord, give me strength to bear my crosses and to offer my sufferings in union with You and Your Mother, Our Lady of Sorrows.

IN TIMES OF SUFFERING

O Lord, sometimes You lift me up to the brightness of visions, and then again You plunge me into the darkness of night and the abyss of my nothingness, and my soul feels as if it were alone in the wilderness. Yet, above all things, I trust in You, Jesus, for You are unchangeable. My moods change, but You are always the same, full of mercy. (1489)

SATURDAY AFTER ASH WEDNESDAY

FAUSTINA: ... I would like to say three words to the soul that is determined to strive for sanctity and to derive fruit; that is to say, benefit from confession. First [word]—complete sincerity and openness.... Second word—humility.... Third word—obedience. (113)

JESUS: **Daughter, when you go to confession, to this fountain of My mercy, the Blood and Water which came forth from My Heart always flows down upon your soul and ennobles it. Every time you go to confession, immerse yourself entirely in My mercy, with great trust, so that I may pour the bounty of My grace upon your soul. When you approach the confessional, know this, that I Myself am waiting there for you. I am only hidden by the priest, but I Myself act in your soul.** (1602)

Thank you, O Lord, for Holy Confession,
For that inexhaustible spring of great mercy,
For that inconceivable fountain of graces
In which sin-tainted souls become purified. (1286)

Dear Lord, give me strength to bear my crosses and to offer my sufferings
in union with You and Your Mother, Our Lady of Sorrows.

IN TIMES OF SUFFERING

... I nestled close to the Most Sacred Heart of Jesus with so much trust
that even if I had the sins of all the damned weighing on my conscience,
I would not have doubted God's mercy but, with a heart crushed to dust,
I would have thrown myself into the abyss of Your mercy. I believe, O
Jesus, that You would not reject me, but would absolve me through the
hand of Your representative. (1318)

FIRST SUNDAY OF LENT

FAUSTINA: Jesus, transform me into another host! I want to be a living
host for You. You are a great and all-powerful Lord; You can grant me
this favor.... O my Jesus, I understand the meaning of "host," the meaning of sacrifice. I desire to be before Your Majesty a living host; that is,
a living sacrifice that daily burns in Your honor. (1826)

JESUS: **You are a living host, pleasing to the Heavenly Father.** (1826)

PRAYER

Throughout this Lent, I am a host in Your hand, Jesus. Make use of me so that You may enter into sinners Yourself. Demand anything You like; no sacrifice will seem too much for me when souls are at stake. (1622)

Dear Lord, give me strength to bear my crosses and to offer my sufferings in union with You and Your Mother, Our Lady of Sorrows.

IN TIMES OF SUFFERING

I am a host in Your hand,
O Jesus, my Creator and Lord,
Silent, hidden, without beauty or charm,
Because all the beauty of my soul is imprinted within me.

I am a host in Your hand, O Divine Priest,
Do with me as You please;
I am totally dependent on Your will, O Lord
Because it is the delight and adornment of my soul.

I am like a white host in Your hand, O God,
I implore You, transform me into Yourself.
May I be wholly hidden in You,
Locked in Your merciful Heart as in Heaven.

I am like a host in Your hand, O Eternal Priest,
May the wafer of my body hide me from human eye;
May Your eye alone measure my love and devotion,
Because my heart is always united with Your Divine Heart.

I am like a sacrificial host in Your hand, O Divine Mediator,
And I burn on the altar of holocaust,
Crushed and ground by suffering like grains of wheat,
And all this for the sake of Your glory, for the salvation of souls.

I am a host abiding in the tabernacle of Your Heart.
I go through life drowned in Your love,
And I fear nothing in the world,
For You Yourself are my shield, my strength, and my defense.

I am a host, laid on the altar of Your Heart,
To burn forever with the fire of love,
For I know that You have lifted me up solely because of Your mercy,
And so I turn all the gifts and graces to Your glory.

I am a host in Your hand, O Judge and Savior.
In the last hour of my life,
May the omnipotence of Your grace lead me to my goal,
May Your compassion on the vessel of mercy become famous. (1629)

FIRST MONDAY OF LENT

FAUSTINA: During Holy Mass, I saw Jesus stretched out on the Cross, and He said to me, **My pupil, have great love for those who cause you suffering. Do good to those who hate you.** I answered, "O my

Master, You see very well that I feel no love for them, and that troubles me." (1628)

JESUS: **I am taking you into My school for the whole of Lent. I want to teach you how to suffer.** I answered, "With You, Lord, I am ready for everything." ... **You are allowed to drink from the cup from which I drink. I give you that exclusive privilege today....** (1626)

You will recognize that you have love if, after having experienced annoyance and contradiction, you do not lose your peace, but pray for those who have made you suffer and wish them well. (1628)

PRAYER

He who knows how to forgive prepares for himself many graces from God. As often as I look upon the cross, so often will I forgive with all my heart. (390)

Oh, how good it is to call on Jesus for help during a conversation. Oh, how good it is, during a moment of peace, to beg for actual graces. I fear most of all this sort of confidential conversation; there is need of much divine light at times like this, in order to speak with profit, both for the other person's soul, and for one's own as well. God, however, comes to our aid; but we have to ask Him for it. Let no one trust too much in his own self. (1495)

Dear Lord, give me strength to bear my crosses and to offer my sufferings in union with You and Your Mother, Our Lady of Sorrows.

IN TIMES OF SUFFERING

I would not know how to suffer without You, O Christ.
Of myself I would not be able to brave adversities.

Alone, I would not have the courage to drink from Your cup;
But You, Lord, are always with me, and You lead me along
  mysterious paths. (1654)

FIRST TUESDAY OF LENT

FAUSTINA: At the beginning of Lent, I asked my confessor for some
   mortification for this time of fast. I was told not to cut down on my
   food but, while eating, to meditate on how the Lord Jesus, on the Cross,
   accepted vinegar and gall. This would be my mortification. I did not
   know that this would be so beneficial to my soul. The benefit is that I
   am meditating constantly on His sorrowful Passion and so, while I am
   eating, I am not preoccupied with what I am eating, but am reflecting
   on my Lord's death. (618)

JESUS: **My daughter, know that your ardent love and the compassion you have for Me were a consolation to Me in the Garden [of
   Olives].** (1664)

PRAYER

Most sweet Jesus, set on fire my love for You and transform me into Yourself.
Divinize me that my deeds may be pleasing to You. May this be accomplished by the power of the Holy Communion which I receive daily. Oh,
how greatly I desire to be wholly transformed into You, O Lord! (1289)

Dear Lord, give me strength to bear my crosses and to offer my sufferings in union with You and Your Mother, Our Lady of Sorrows.

IN TIMES OF SUFFERING

Today, I received some oranges. When the sister had left, I thought to myself, "Should I eat the oranges instead of doing penance and mortifying myself during Holy Lent? After all, I am feeling a bit better." Then I heard a voice in my soul: **My daughter, you please Me more by eating the oranges out of obedience and love of Me than by fasting and mortifying yourself of your own will.** (1023)

It occurred to me to take my medicine, not by the spoonful, but just a little at a time, because it was expensive. Instantly, I heard a voice, **My daughter, I do not like such conduct. Accept with gratitude everything I give you through the superiors, and in this way you will please Me more.** (1381)

FIRST WEDNESDAY OF LENT

FAUSTINA: I want to live in the spirit of faith. I accept everything that comes my way as given me by the loving will of God, who sincerely desires my happiness. And so I will accept with submission and gratitude everything that God sends me. I will pay no attention to the voice of nature and to the promptings of self-love.

Before each important action, I will stop to consider for a moment what relationship it has to eternal life and what may be the main reason for my undertaking it: is it for the glory of God, or for the good of my own soul, or for the good of the souls of others? If my heart says yes, then I will not swerve from carrying out the given action, unmindful of either obstacles or sacrifices. I will not be frightened into abandoning my intention. It is enough for me to know that it is pleasing to God. On the other hand, if I learn that the action has nothing in common with what I have just mentioned, I will try to elevate it to a loftier sphere by means of a good intention. And if I learn that something flows from my self-love, I will cancel it out right from the start. (1549)

JESUS: **O how pleasing to Me is living faith!** (1420)**. Tell all ... that I demand that they live in the spirit of faith....** (353)

PRAYER

I fervently beg the Lord to strengthen my faith, so that in my drab, everyday life I will not be guided by human dispositions, but by those of the spirit. Oh, how everything drags man towards the earth! But lively faith maintains the soul in the higher regions and assigns self-love its proper place; that is to say, the lowest one. (210)

Dear Lord, give me strength to bear my crosses and to offer my sufferings in union with You and Your Mother, Our Lady of Sorrows.

IN TIMES OF SUFFERING

I often ask the Lord Jesus for an intellect enlightened by faith. I express this to the Lord in these words: "Jesus, give me an intellect, a great intellect, for this only, that I may understand You better; because the better I get to know You, the more ardently will I love You. Jesus, I ask You for a powerful intellect, that I may understand divine and lofty matters. Jesus, give me a keen intellect with which I will get to know Your Divine Essence and Your indwelling, Triune life. Give my intellect these capacities and aptitudes by means of your special grace." (1474)

FIRST THURSDAY OF LENT

FAUSTINA: Today I felt more ill, but Jesus has given me many more opportunities on this day to practice virtue. It so happened that I was busier than usual, and the sister in charge of the kitchen made it clear to me how irritated she was that I had come late for dinner, although it was quite impossible for me to have come sooner. At any rate, I felt so unwell that I had to ask Mother Superior to allow me to lie down. I went to ask Sister N. to take my place, and again I got a scolding: "What is this, Sister, you're so exhausted that you're going back to bed again! Confound you with all this lying in bed!" I put up with all that, but that wasn't the end. I still had to ask the sister who was in charge of the sick to bring me my meal. When I told her this, she burst out of the chapel into the corridor after me to give me a piece of her mind: "Why on earth are you going to bed, Sister, etc.,..." I asked her not to bother bringing me anything.

I am writing all this very briefly because it is not my intention to write about such things, and I am doing so merely to dissuade souls from treating others in this way, for this is displeasing to the Lord. In a suffering soul we should see Jesus Crucified, and not a loafer or burden on the community. A soul who suffers with submission to the will of God draws down more blessings on the whole convent than all the working sisters. Poor indeed is a convent where there are no sick sisters. God often grants many and great graces out of regard for the souls who are suffering, and He withholds many punishments solely because of the suffering souls. (1268)

JESUS: **If someone causes you trouble, think what good you can do for that person who caused you to suffer.** (1760)

PRAYER

"Jesus!" I called out with all the strength of my soul. (173)

Dear Lord, give me strength to bear my crosses and to offer my sufferings in union with You and Your Mother, Our Lady of Sorrows.

IN TIMES OF SUFFERING

Jesus, may Your pure and healthy blood circulate in my ailing organism, and may Your pure and healthy body transform my weak body, and may a healthy and vigorous life throb within me, if it is truly Your holy will that I should set about the work in question; and this will be a clear sign of Your holy will for me. (1089)

FIRST FRIDAY OF LENT

FAUSTINA: When I make the Way of the Cross, I am deeply moved at the twelfth station. Here I reflect on the omnipotence of God's mercy which passed through the Heart of Jesus. In this open wound of the Heart of Jesus I enclose all poor humans ... and those individuals whom I love, as often as I make the Way of the Cross. From that Fount of Mercy issued the two rays; that is, the Blood and the Water. With the immensity of their grace they flood the whole world.... (1309)

JESUS: **My daughter, try your best to make the Stations of the Cross ... and if you are not able to make the Stations of the Cross, then at least step into the chapel for a moment and adore, in the Blessed Sacrament, My Heart, which is full of mercy; and should you be unable to step into the chapel, immerse yourself in prayer there where you happen to be, if only for a very brief instant. I claim veneration for My mercy from every creature, but above all from you, since it is to you that I have given the most profound understanding of this mystery.** (1572)

PRAYER

O my most compassionate Creator, I want to give you worship on behalf of all creatures and all inanimate creation; ... (1749). May Your mercy be glorified, O Lord; we will praise it for endless ages. And the angels were amazed at the greatness of the mercy which You have shown for mankind.... (1743)

Dear Lord, give me strength to bear my crosses and to offer my sufferings in union with You and Your Mother, Our Lady of Sorrows.

IN TIMES OF SUFFERING

Suffering is a great grace; through suffering the soul becomes like the Savior; in suffering love becomes crystallized; the greater the suffering, the purer the love. (57)

My Jesus, You suffice me for everything else in the world. Although the sufferings are severe, You sustain me. Although the times of loneliness are terrible, You make them sweet for me. Although the weakness is great, You change it into power for me. (1655)

FIRST SATURDAY OF LENT

FAUSTINA: Faithful submission to the will of God, always and everywhere, in all events and circumstances of life, gives great glory to God. Such submission to the will of God carries more weight with Him than long fasts, mortifications and the most severe penances. Oh, how great is the reward for one act of loving submission to the will of God! As I write, my soul is enraptured at the thought of how much God loves it and of the peace that my soul already enjoys, here on earth. (724)

JESUS: **My daughter ... it is when you submit yourself to My will that you give Me the greatest glory and draw down upon yourself a sea of blessings. I would not take such special delight in you if you were not living by my will.** (954)

PRAYER

It is with love that I abandon myself to Your most wise decrees, O God, and Your will, O Lord, is my daily nourishment (1145). I abandon myself entirely to the action of Your grace. Let Your will be accomplished entirely in me, O Lord. (1326)

Dear Lord, give me strength to bear my crosses and to offer my sufferings in union with You and Your Mother, Our Lady of Sorrows.

IN TIMES OF SUFFERING

It is impossible for one to please God without obeying His holy will. Then the Mother of God said, ... *My daughter, I strongly recommend that you faithfully fulfill all God's wishes, for that is most pleasing in His holy eyes. I very much desire that you distinguish yourself in this faithfulness in accomplishing God's will. Put the will of God before all sacrifices and holocausts.* While the heavenly Mother was talking to me, a deep understanding of this will of God was entering my soul. (1244)

SECOND SUNDAY OF LENT

FAUSTINA: Now that I have difficulty sleeping at night, because my suffering won't allow it, I visit all the churches and chapels and, if only for a brief moment, I make an act of adoration before the Blessed Sacrament.... I then pray for certain priests who proclaim and glorify The Divine Mercy. I also pray for the intentions of the Holy Father and to obtain mercy for sinners—such are my nights. (1501)

Today, I saw the Lord in great beauty, and he said to me, **My loving host, pray for priests,...** (980)

PRAYER

O priests, you bright candles enlightening human souls, let your brightness never be dimmed. (75)

Dear Lord, give me strength to bear my crosses and to offer my sufferings in union with You and Your Mother, Our Lady of Sorrows.

IN TIMES OF SUFFERING

I thank God for this illness and these physical discomforts, because I have time to converse with the Lord Jesus. It is my delight to spend long hours at the feet of the hidden God, and the hours pass like minutes as I lose track of time. I feel that a fire is burning within me, and I understand no other life but that of sacrifice, which flows from pure love. (784)

SECOND MONDAY OF LENT

FAUSTINA: Where there is genuine virtue, there must be sacrifice as well; one's whole life must be a sacrifice. It is only by means of sacrifice that souls can become useful. It is my self-sacrifice which, in my relationship with my neighbor, can give glory to God, but God's love must flow through this sacrifice, because everything is concentrated in this love and takes its value from it. (1358)

JESUS: **This firm resolution to become a saint is extremely pleasing to Me. I bless your efforts and will give you opportunities to sanctify yourself. Be watchful that you lose no opportunity that My providence offers you for sanctification. If you do not succeed in taking advantage of an opportunity, do not lose your peace, but humble yourself profoundly before Me and, with great trust, immerse yourself completely in My mercy. In this way, you gain more than you have lost, because more favor is granted to a humble soul than the soul itself asks for.** (1361)

PRAYER

My Jesus, penetrate me through and through so that I might be able to reflect You in my whole life. Divinize me so that my deeds may have supernatural value. Grant that I may have love, compassion and mercy for every soul without exception. O my Jesus, each of Your saints reflects one of Your virtues; I desire to reflect Your compassionate heart, full of mercy; I want to glorify it. Let Your mercy, O Jesus, be impressed upon my heart and soul like a seal, and this will be my badge in this and the future life. Glorifying Your mercy is the exclusive task of my life. (1242)

Dear Lord, give me strength to bear my crosses and to offer my sufferings in union with You and Your Mother, Our Lady of Sorrows.

IN TIMES OF SUFFERING

When I see that the burden is beyond my strength, I do not consider or analyze it or probe into it, but I run like a child to the Heart of Jesus and say only one word to Him: "You can do all things." And then I keep silent, because I know that Jesus Himself will intervene in the matter, and as for me, instead of tormenting myself, I use that time to love Him. (1033)

SECOND TUESDAY OF LENT

FAUSTINA: O my Jesus, how very easy it is to become holy; all that is needed is a bit of good will. If Jesus sees this little bit of good will in the soul, He hurries to give Himself to the soul, and nothing can stop Him, neither shortcomings nor falls — absolutely nothing. Jesus is anxious to help that soul, and if it is faithful to this grace from God, it can very soon attain the highest holiness possible for a creature here on earth. God is very generous and does not deny His grace to anyone. Indeed, He gives more than what we ask of Him. Faithfulness to the inspirations of the Holy Spirit — that is the shortest route. (291)

JESUS: **Be not afraid of your Savior; O sinful soul. I make the first move to come to you, for I know that by yourself you are unable to lift yourself to me. Child, do not run away from your Father; be willing to talk openly with your God of mercy who wants to speak words of pardon and lavish his graces on you. How dear your soul is to Me! I have inscribed your name upon My hand; you are engraved as a deep wound in My Heart.** (1485)

PRAYER

O Spirit of God, Director of the soul, wise is he whom You have trained! But for the Spirit of God to act in the soul, peace and recollection are needed. (145)

Come, Holy Spirit, fill the hearts of Your faithful and enkindle in them the first of Your love.

Send forth Your Spirit and they shall be created. And You shall renew the face of the earth.

O God, who instructed the hearts of the faithful by the light of the Holy Spirit, grant that by that same Spirit we may be truly wise and ever to rejoice in His consolation. Through Christ Our Lord. Amen.

Dear Lord, give me strength to bear my crosses and to offer my sufferings in union with You and Your Mother, Our Lady of Sorrows.

IN TIMES OF SUFFERING

At the beginning of my religious life, suffering and adversities frightened and disheartened me. So I prayed continuously, asking Jesus to strengthen me and to grant me the power of his Holy Spirit that I might carry out

His holy will in all things, because from the beginning I have been aware of my weakness. I know very well what I am of myself, because for this purpose Jesus has opened the eyes of my soul; I am an abyss of misery, and hence I understand that whatever good there is in my soul consists solely of His holy grace. The knowledge of my own misery allows me, at the same time, to know the immensity of Your mercy. In my own interior life, I am looking with one eye at the abyss of my misery and baseness, and with the other, at the abyss of Your mercy, O God. (56)

SECOND WEDNESDAY OF LENT

FAUSTINA: O you small, everyday sacrifices, you are to me like wild flowers which I strew over the feet of my beloved Jesus. I sometimes compare these trifles to the heroic virtues and that is because their enduring nature demands heroism. (208)

JESUS: **You are not living for yourself but for souls, and other souls will profit from your sufferings. Your prolonged suffering will give them light and strength to accept My will.** (67)

PRAYER

I make a voluntary offering of myself for the conversion of sinners, especially for those souls who have lost hope in God's mercy. (309)

Dear Lord, give me strength to bear my crosses and to offer my sufferings in union with You and Your Mother, Our Lady of Sorrows.

IN TIMES OF SUFFERING

Jesus, I thank You for the little daily crosses, for opposition to my endeavors, for the hardships of communal life, for the misinterpretation of my intentions, for humiliations at the hands of others, for the harsh way in which we are treated, for false suspicions, for poor health and loss of strength, for self-denial, for dying to myself, for lack of recognition in everything, for the upsetting of all my plans.

Thank You, Jesus, for interior sufferings, for dryness of spirit, for terrors, fears and uncertainties, for the darkness and the deep interior night, for temptations and various ordeals, for torments too difficult to describe, especially for those which no one will understand, for the hour of death with its fierce struggle and all its bitterness. (343)

SECOND THURSDAY OF LENT

FAUSTINA: The Lord Jesus appeared as He was during the scourging. In His hands He was holding a white garment with which He clothed me and a cord with which He girded me, and He covered me with a red cloak like the one He was clothed with during His Passion and a veil of the same color and He said to me,

JESUS: **Fix your eyes upon Me and live according to what you see. I desire that you penetrate into My spirit more deeply and understand that I am meek and humble of heart.** (526)

PRAYER

O humility, lovely flower, I see how few souls possess you. Is it because you are so beautiful and at the same time so difficult to attain? O yes, it is both the one and the other. Even God takes great pleasure in her. The floodgates of heaven are open to a humble soul, and a sea of graces flows down upon her. O how beautiful is a humble soul! From her heart, as from a censer, rises a varied and most pleasing fragrance which breaks through the skies and reaches God Himself, filling His Most Sacred Heart with joy. God refuses nothing to such a soul; she is all-powerful and influences the destiny of the whole world. God raises such a soul up to His very throne, and the more she humbles herself, the more God stoops down to her, pursuing her with His graces and accompanying her at every moment with His omnipotence. Such a soul is most deeply united with God. O humility, strike deep roots in my whole being. O Virgin most pure, but also most humble, help me to attain deep humility. (1306)

Dear Lord, give me strength to bear my crosses and to offer my sufferings in union with You and Your Mother, Our Lady of Sorrows.

IN TIMES OF SUFFERING

A humble soul does not trust itself, but places all its confidence in God. (593)

Jesus, Eternal Light, enlighten my mind, strengthen my will, inflame my heart and be with me as You have promised, for without You I am nothing. You know, Jesus, how weak I am. I do not need to tell You this, for You Yourself know perfectly well how wretched I am. It is in You that all my strength lies. (495)

SECOND FRIDAY OF LENT

FAUSTINA: It is no easy thing to bear sufferings joyfully, especially those which are unmerited. Fallen nature rebels, and although the intellect and will are above suffering, because they are able to do good to those who inflict suffering on them, nevertheless the emotions raise a lot of noise and, like restless spirits, attack the intellect and will. But when they see they cannot do anything by themselves, they quiet down and submit to the intellect and will. Like some kind of hideousness, they rush in and stir up a row, bent on making one obey them alone so long as they are not curbed by the intellect and will. (1152)

JESUS: **Do not be surprised that you are sometimes unjustly accused. I Myself first drank this cup of undeserved suffering for love of you.** (289)

PRAYER

O Jesus, how deeply it hurts the soul when it is always trying to be sincere and they accuse it of hypocrisy and behave with mistrust toward it. O Jesus, You also suffered like this to make satisfaction to Your Father. (200)

Dear Lord, give me strength to bear my crosses and to offer my sufferings in union with You and Your Mother, Our Lady of Sorrows.

IN TIMES OF SUFFERING

Although it is not easy to live in constant agony,
To be nailed to the cross of various pains,
Still, I am inflamed with love by loving,
And like a Seraph I love God, though I am but weakness.

Oh, great is the soul that, midst suffering,
Stands faithfully by God and does His will
And remains uncomforted midst great rainbows and storms,
For God's pure love sweetens her fate.

It is no great thing to love God in prosperity
And thank Him when all goes well,
But rather to adore Him midst great adversities
And love Him for His own sake and place one's hope in Him.

When the soul is in the shadows of Gethsemane,
All alone in the bitterness of pain,
It ascends toward the heights of Jesus,
And though ever drinking bitterness—it is not sad.

When the soul does the will of the Most High God,
Even amidst constant pain and torments,

Having pressed its lips to the chalice proffered,
It becomes mighty, and nothing will daunt it.

Though tortured, it repeats: Your will be done,
Patiently awaiting the moment of its transfiguration,
For, though in deepest darkness, it hears the voice of Jesus: You are Mine,
And this it will know fully when the veil falls. (995)

SECOND SATURDAY OF LENT

OUR LADY TO FAUSTINA: *I desire, My dearly beloved daughter, that you practice the three virtues that are dearest to Me — and most pleasing to God. The first is humility, humility, and once again humility; the second virtue, purity; the third virtue, love of God. As My daughter, you must especially radiate with these virtues.* (1415)

FAUSTINA: Now I understand why there are so few saints; it is because so few souls are deeply humble. (1306) ... I will practice the three virtues recommended to me by the Mother of God: humility, purity and love of God, accepting with profound submission to the will of God everything that He will send me. (1624)

JESUS: **My daughter, let three virtues adorn you in a particular way; humility, purity of intention and love.** (1779)

PRAYER

If there is a truly happy soul upon earth, it can only be a truly humble soul. (593)

O Virgin most pure, but also most humble, help me to attain deep humility. (1306) O radiant Virgin, pure as crystal, all immersed in God, I offer You my spiritual life; arrange everything that it may be pleasing to Your Son. (844)

Dear Lord, give me strength to bear my crosses and to offer my sufferings in union with You and Your Mother, Our Lady of Sorrows.

IN TIMES OF SUFFERING

The more I imitate the Mother of God, the more deeply I get to know God. (843)

O Mary, my Mother and my Lady, I offer You my soul, my body, my life and my death, and all that will follow it. I place everything in Your hands. O my Mother, cover my soul with Your virginal mantle and grant me the grace of purity of heart, soul and body. Defend me with Your power against all enemies, and especially against those who hide their malice behind the mask of virtue. O lovely lily! You are for me a mirror, O my Mother! (79)

THIRD SUNDAY OF LENT

SOUL/FAUSTINA: What should I do when I am ignored and rejected by people, especially by those on whom I had a right to count in times of greatest need? (1487)

JESUS: **My child, make the resolution never to rely on people. Entrust yourself completely to My will saying, "Not as I want, but according to Your will, O God, let it be done unto me." These words, spoken from the depths of one's heart, can raise a soul to the summit of sanctity in a short time. In such a soul I delight. Such a soul gives Me glory. Such a soul fills heaven with the fragrance of her virtue. But understand that the strength by which you bear sufferings comes from frequent Communions. So approach this fountain of mercy often, to draw with the vessel of trust whatever you need. (1487)**

PRAYER

Thank You, Lord, for Your goodness in remaining with us in this exile as the God of mercy and blessing us with the radiance of Your compassion and goodness. It is through the light of Your mercy that I have come to understand how much You love me. (1487).

Dear Lord, give me strength to bear my crosses and to offer my sufferings in union with You and Your Mother, Our Lady of Sorrows.

IN TIMES OF SUFFERING

Every morning during meditation, I prepare myself for the whole day's struggle. Holy Communion assures me that I will win the victory; and so it is. I fear the day when I do not receive Holy Communion. This Bread of the Strong gives me all the strength I need to carry on my mission and the courage to do whatever the Lord asks of me. The courage and strength that are in me are not of me, but of Him who lives in me — it is the Eucharist. (91)

ACT OF SPIRITUAL COMMUNION BY ST. ALPHONSUS LIGUORI

My Jesus, I believe that You are truly present in the Most Holy Sacrament. I love You above all things, and I desire to receive You into my soul. Since I cannot at this moment receive You sacramentally, come at least spiritually into my heart. I embrace You as being already there and unite myself wholly to You. Never permit me to be separated from You. Amen.

THIRD MONDAY OF LENT

FAUSTINA: When I am asleep I offer Him every beat of my heart; when I awaken I immerse myself in Him without saying a word. When I awaken I adore the Holy Trinity for a short while and thank God for having deigned to give me yet another day, that the mystery of the incarnation of His Son may once more be repeated in me, and that once again His sorrowful Passion may unfold before my eyes. I then try to make it easier for Jesus to pass through me to other souls. I go everywhere with Jesus; His presence accompanies me everywhere. (486)

JESUS: ... do not forget, My disciple, that you are a disciple of a cruci-fied Master. (1513)

PRAYER

O Most Holy Trinity! As many times as I breathe, as many times as my heart beats, as many times as my blood pulsates through my body, so many thousand times do I want to glorify Your mercy. (163)

Thank You, O Holy Trinity, for the vastness of the graces
Which You have lavished on me unceasingly through life.
My gratitude will intensify as the eternal dawn rises,
When, for the first time, I sing to Your glory. (1286)

Dear Lord, give me strength to bear my crosses and to offer my sufferings in union with You and Your Mother, Our Lady of Sorrows.

IN TIMES OF SUFFERING

Jesus, source of life, sanctify me. O my strength, fortify me. My Com-mander, fight for me. Only light of my soul, enlighten me. My Master, guide me. I entrust myself to You as a little child does to its mother's love. Even if all things were to conspire against me, and even if the ground were to give way under my feet, I would be at peace close to Your Heart. You are always a most tender mother to me, and You surpass all mothers.

I will sing of my pain to You by my silence, and You will understand me beyond any utterance.... (1490)

THIRD TUESDAY OF LENT

FAUSTINA: Silence is a sword in the spiritual struggle. A talkative soul will never attain sanctity. The sword of silence will cut off everything that would like to cling to the soul. We are sensitive to words and quickly want to answer back, without taking any regard as to whether it is God's will that we should speak (477). The Lord gave me to know how displeased He is with a talkative soul. (1008)

JESUS: **I find no rest in such a soul. The constant din tires Me, and in the midst of it the soul cannot discern My voice.** (1008)

PRAYER

Oh, how good it is that Jesus will judge us according to our conscience and not according to people's talk and judgments. O inconceivable goodness, I see You full of goodness in the very act of judgment (1470). O Blessed Host, support me and seal my lips against all murmuring and complaint. When I am silent, I know I shall be victorious. (896)

Dear Lord, give me strength to bear my crosses and to offer my sufferings in union with You and Your Mother, Our Lady of Sorrows.

IN TIMES OF SUFFERING

Today, the Majesty of God is surrounding me. There is no way that I can help myself to prepare better. I am thoroughly enwrapped in God. My soul is being inflamed by His love. I only know that I love and am loved. That is enough for me. I am trying my best to be faithful throughout the day to the Holy Spirit and to fulfill His demands. I am trying my best for interior silence in order to be able to hear His voice.... (1828)

O Lord, You who penetrate my whole being and the most secret depths of my soul, You see that I desire You alone and long only for the fulfillment of Your holy will, paying no heed to difficulties or sufferings or humiliations or to what others might think. (1360)

THIRD WEDNESDAY OF LENT

FAUSTINA: Jesus, do not leave me alone in suffering. (1489)

JESUS: **My daughter, do not be afraid of what will happen to you. I will give you nothing beyond your strength. You know the power of My grace; let that be enough.** (1491)

PRAYER

Do with me as You please, Lord, only give me the grace to be able to love You in every event and circumstance, Lord, do not lessen my cup of bitterness, only give me strength that I may be able to drink it all. (1489)

Dear Lord, give me strength to bear my crosses and to offer my sufferings in union with You and Your Mother, Our Lady of Sorrows.

IN TIMES OF SUFFERING

In the evening, when I entered the small chapel, I heard these words in my soul: **My daughter, consider these words: "And being in agony, he prayed more earnestly."** When I started to think about them more deeply, much light streamed into my soul. I learned how much we need perseverance in prayer and that our salvation often depends on such difficult prayer. (157)

THIRD THURSDAY OF LENT

SOUL/FAUSTINA: O Lord, now I see all my ingratitude and Your goodness. You were pursuing me with Your grace, while I was frustrating Your benevolence. I see that I deserve the depths of hell for spurning Your graces. (1486)

JESUS: **Do not be absorbed in your misery—you are still too weak to speak of it—but, rather, gaze on My Heart filled with goodness, and be imbued with My sentiments. Strive for meekness and humility; be merciful to others, as I am to you; and, when you feel your strength failing, if you come to the fountain of mercy to fortify your soul, you will not grow weary on your journey.** (1486)

PRAYER

O Lord, I am inundated with Your grace. I sense that a new life has entered into me and, above all, I feel Your love in my heart. That is enough for me. O Lord, I will glorify the omnipotence of Your mercy for all eternity. Encouraged by Your goodness, I will confide to You all the sorrows of my heart. (1486)

Dear Lord, give me strength to bear my crosses and to offer my sufferings in union with You and Your Mother, Our Lady of Sorrows.

IN TIMES OF SUFFERING

Jesus, Friend of a lonely heart, You are my heaven. You are my peace. You are my salvation, You are my serenity in moments of struggle and amidst an ocean of doubts. You are the bright ray that lights up the path of my life. You are everything to a lonely soul. You understand the soul even though it remains silent. You know our weaknesses, and like a good physician, You comfort and heal, sparing us sufferings—expert that You are. (247)

THIRD FRIDAY OF LENT

FAUSTINA: Today, I experienced a great suffering during the visit of our sisters. I learned of something that hurt me terribly, but I controlled myself so that the sisters didn't notice anything. For some time, the pain was tearing my heart apart, but all that is for the sake of poor sinners.... O Jesus, for poor sinners.... Jesus, my strength, stay close to me, help me.... (875)

JESUS: **... pray for those who have made you suffer and wish them well.** (1628)

PRAYER

I do not lose inner peace or exterior balance, and this discourages my adversaries. Patience in adversity gives power to the soul. (607)

Dear Lord, give me the strength to bear my crosses in peace and patience and to offer up my sufferings in union with You and Your Mother.

IN TIMES OF SUFFERING

Jesus-Host, if You Yourself did not sustain me, I would not be able to persevere on the cross. I would not be able to endure so much suffering. But the power of Your grace maintains me on a higher level and makes my sufferings meritorious. You give me strength always to move forward and to gain heaven by force and to have love in my heart for those from whom I suffer adversities and contempt. With Your grace one can do all things. (1620)

THIRD SATURDAY OF LENT

FAUSTINA: I heard the rustling of garments and saw the most holy Mother of God in a most beautiful radiance. Her white garment was girdled with a blue sash. She said to me, *You give Me great joy when you adore The Holy Trinity for the graces and privileges which were accorded Me.* (564)

JESUS: **You are Our dwelling place.** (451)

PRAYER

Be adored, O Most Holy Trinity, now and for all time. Be adored in all Your works and all Your creatures. May the greatness of Your mercy be admired and glorified, O God. (5)

O Holy Trinity, in whom is contained the inner life of God, the Father, the Son, and the Holy Spirit, eternal joy, inconceivable depth of love, poured out upon all creatures and constituting their happiness, honor and glory be to Your holy name forever and ever. Amen. (525)

Dear God, give me the strength to bear my crosses patiently and to offer up my sufferings in union with my Crucified Savior and His Mother, Our Lady of Sorrows.

IN TIMES OF SUFFERING

We should often pray to the Holy Spirit for this grace of prudence. Prudence consists in discretion, rational reflection and courageous resolution. The final decision is always up to us. (1106)

O Holy Trinity, Eternal God, I thank You for allowing me to know the greatness and the various degrees of glory to which souls attain. Oh, what a great difference of depth in the knowledge of God there is between one degree and another! Oh, if people could only know this! O my God, if I were thereby able to attain one more degree, I would gladly suffer all the torments of the martyrs put together. Truly, all those torments seem as nothing to me compared with the glory that is awaiting us for all eternity. O Lord, immerse my soul in the ocean of Your divinity and grant me the grace of knowing You; for the better I know You, the more I desire You, and the more my love for You grows. I feel in my soul an unfathomable abyss which only God can fill. I lose myself in Him as a drop does in the ocean. The Lord has inclined himself to my misery like a ray of the sun upon a barren and rocky desert. And yet, under the influence of His rays, my soul has become covered with verdure, flowers, and fruit, and has become a beautiful garden for His repose. (605)

FOURTH SUNDAY OF LENT

FAUSTINA: The glory of the Divine Mercy is resounding, even now, in spite of the efforts of its enemies and of Satan himself, who has a great hatred for God's mercy. This work will snatch a great number of souls from him, and that is why the spirit of darkness sometimes tempts good people violently, so that they may hinder the work.... The enemy's greatest efforts will not thwart the smallest detail of what the Lord has decreed. (1659)

JESUS: **Do not fear; I am with you.** (129)

PRAYER

Today I have fought a battle with the spirits of darkness over one soul (812). How terribly ugly Satan is! (540). O merciful God, You do not despise us, but lavish Your graces on us continuously. You make us fit to enter Your kingdom, and in Your goodness You grant that human beings may fill the places vacated by the ungrateful angels. O God of great mercy, who turned Your sacred gaze away from the rebellious angels and turned it upon contrite man, praise and glory be to Your unfathomable mercy, O God who do not despise the lowly heart. (1339)

Dear God, give me the strength to bear my crosses patiently and to offer up my sufferings in union with my Crucified Savior and His Mother, Our Lady of Sorrows.

IN TIMES OF SUFFERING

O merciful Jesus, stretched on the cross, be mindful of the hour of our death. O most merciful Heart of Jesus, opened with a lance, shelter me at the last moment of my life. O Blood and Water, which gushed forth from the Heart of Jesus as a fount of unfathomable mercy for me at the hour of my death, O dying Jesus, Hostage of mercy, avert the Divine wrath at the hour of my death. (813)

FOURTH MONDAY OF LENT

FAUSTINA: Jesus again gave me a few directives. (1560)

JESUS: **First, do not fight against a temptation by yourself, but disclose it to the confessor at once, and then the temptation will lose all its** force. Second, during these ordeals do not lose your peace; live in My presence; ask My Mother and the Saints for help. Third, have the certitude that I am looking at you and supporting you. Fourth, do not fear either struggles of the soul or any temptations, because I am supporting you; if only you are willing to fight, know that the victory is always on your side. Fifth, know that by fighting bravely you give Me great glory and amass merits for yourself. Temptation gives you a chance to show Me your fidelity. (1560)

PRAYER

O Lord, save me Yourself, for I perish. Be my Savior. (1486)

Dear God, give me the strength to bear my crosses patiently and to offer up my sufferings in union with my Crucified Savior and His Mother, Our Lady of Sorrows.

IN TIMES OF SUFFERING

JESUS: **Fight like a knight, so I can reward you** (1760). **Be at peace** (145). **Do not be unduly fearful, because you are not alone.** (1760)

FAUSTINA: Saint Joseph urged me to have a constant devotion to him. He himself told me to recite three prayers [the Our Father, the Hail Mary, and the Glory Be] and the *Memorare* once every day. He looked at me with great kindness and gave me to know how much he is supporting this work [of mercy]. He has promised me this special help and protection. I recite the requested prayers every day and feel his special protection. (1203)

FOURTH TUESDAY OF LENT

FAUSTINA: My sister [Wanda] came to see me today. When she told me of her plans, I was horror-stricken. How is such a thing possible? Such a beautiful little soul before the Lord, and yet, great darkness had come over her, and she did not know how to help herself. She had a dark view of everything. The good God entrusted her to my care, and for two weeks I was able to work with her. But how many sacrifices this soul cost me is known only to God. For no other soul did I bring so many sacrifices and sufferings and prayers before the throne of God as I did for her soul. I felt that I had forced God to grant her grace. When I reflect on all this, I see that it was truly a miracle. Now I can see how much power intercessory prayer has before God. (202)

JESUS: **When you say this prayer, with a contrite heart and with faith on behalf of some sinner, I will give him the grace of conversion. This is the prayer:** (186)

> **"O Blood and Water,**
> **which gushed forth from the Heart of Jesus**
> **as a fount of Mercy for us, I trust in You."** (187)

PRAYER

O Most Holy Trinity dwelling in my heart, I beg You: grant the grace of conversion to as many souls as the [number of] stitches that I will make today with this crochet hook. (961)

Dear God, give me the strength to bear my crosses patiently and to offer up my sufferings in union with my Crucified Savior and His Mother, Our Lady of Sorrows.

IN TIMES OF SUFFERING

I saw that my suffering and prayer shackled Satan and snatched many souls from his clutches (1465). My sacrifice is nothing in itself, but when I join it to the sacrifice of Jesus Christ, it becomes all-powerful and has the power to appease divine wrath. (482).

O Jesus, shield me with Your mercy and also judge me leniently.... (1093)

FOURTH WEDNESDAY OF LENT

FAUSTINA: Once after an adoration for our country, a pain pierced my soul and I began to pray in this way: "Most merciful Jesus, I beseech You through the intercession of Your Saints, and especially the intercession of Your dearest Mother who nurtured You from childhood, bless my native land. I beg You, Jesus, look not on our sins, but on the tears of little children, on the hunger and cold they suffer. Jesus, for the sake of these innocent ones, grant me the grace that I am asking of you for my country."

JESUS: **You see, My daughter, what great compassion I have for them. Know that it is they who uphold the world.** (286)

Help me, happy inhabitants of the heavenly homeland, so that your sister may not falter on the way. (886)

IN TIMES OF SUFFERING

Sorrow will not establish itself in a heart which loves the will of God. My heart, longing for God, feels the whole misery of exile. I keep going forward bravely—though my feet become wounded—to my homeland and, on the way, I nourish myself on the will of God. It is my food.... Although the desert is fearful, I walk with lifted head and eyes fixed on the sun; that is to say, on the merciful Heart of Jesus. (886)

FOURTH THURSDAY OF LENT

SOUL/FAUSTINA: Lord, I doubt that you will pardon my numerous sins; my misery fills me with fright.... I invite you to my heart. (1485)

JESUS: **My child, do you fear the God of mercy? My holiness does not prevent Me from being merciful. Behold, for you I have established a throne of mercy on earth—the tabernacle—and from this throne I desire to enter your heart. I am not surrounded by a retinue or guards. You can come to me at any moment, at any time; I want to speak to you and desire to grant you grace. (1485)**

PRAYER

O great, incomprehensible God,
Who have deigned to abase Yourself so,
Humbly I adore You
And beg You in Your goodness to save me. (1231)

Dear God, give me the strength to bear my crosses patiently and to offer up my sufferings in union with my Crucified Savior and His Mother, Our Lady of Sorrows.

IN TIMES OF SUFFERING

You have conquered, O Lord, my stony heart with Your goodness. In trust and humility I approach the tribunal of Your mercy, where You Yourself absolve me by the hand of your representative. O Lord, I feel Your grace and Your peace filling my poor soul. I feel overwhelmed by Your mercy, O lord. You forgive me, which is more than I dared to hope for or could imagine. Your goodness surpasses all my desires. And now, filled with gratitude for so many graces, I invite You to my heart. I wandered, like a prodigal child gone astray; but you did not cease to be my Father. Increase Your mercy toward me, for You see how weak I am. (1485)

FOURTH FRIDAY OF LENT

FAUSTINA: O my Jesus, you know what efforts are needed to live sincerely and unaffectedly with those from whom our nature flees, or with those who, deliberately or not, have made us suffer. Humanly speaking, this is impossible. At such times more than at others, I try to discover the Lord Jesus in such a person and for this same Jesus, I do everything for such people. In such acts, love is pure, and such practice of love gives the soul endurance and strength. (766)

JESUS: **I am giving you three ways of exercising mercy toward your neighbor: the first — by deed, the second — by word, the third — by prayer. In these three degrees is contained the fullness of mercy, and it is an unquestionable proof of love for Me. . . . You must not shrink from this or try to excuse or absolve yourself from it.** (742)

PRAYER

I want to be completely transformed into Your mercy and to be Your living reflection, O Lord. May the greatest of all divine attributes, that of Your unfathomable mercy, pass through my heart and soul to my neighbor.

Help me, O Lord, that my eyes may be merciful, so that I may never suspect or judge from appearances, but look for what is beautiful in my neighbors' souls and come to their rescue.

Help me, O Lord, that my ears may be merciful, so that I may give heed to my neighbors' needs and not be indifferent to their pains and moanings.

Help me, O Lord, that my tongue may be merciful, so that I should never speak negatively of my neighbor, but have a word of comfort and forgiveness for all.

Help me, O Lord, that my hands may be merciful and filled with good deeds, so that I may do only good to my neighbors and take upon myself the more difficult and toilsome tasks.

Help me, that my feet may be merciful, so that I may hurry to assist my neighbor, overcoming my own fatigue and weariness.

Help me, O Lord, that my heart may be merciful so that I myself may feel all the sufferings of my neighbor. (163)

Dear God, give me the strength to bear my crosses patiently and to offer up my sufferings in union with my Crucified Savior and His Mother, Our Lady of Sorrows.

IN TIMES OF SUFFERING

In order to purify a soul, Jesus uses whatever instruments He likes. My soul underwent a complete abandonment on the part of creatures; often my best intentions were misinterpreted by the sisters, a type of suffering which is most painful; but God allows it, and we must accept it because in this way we become more like Jesus. (38)

FOURTH SATURDAY OF LENT

FAUSTINA: My Jesus, despite Your graces, I see and feel all my misery. I begin my day with battle and end it with battle. As soon as I conquer one obstacle, ten more appear to take its place. But I am not worried, because I know that this is the time of struggle, not peace. When the burden of the battle becomes too much for me, I throw myself like a child into the arms of the heavenly Father and trust I will not perish. O my Jesus, how prone I am to evil, and this forces me to be constantly vigilant. But I do not lose heart. I trust God's grace, which abounds in the worst misery. (606)

JESUS: **Daughter, give Me your misery, because it is your exclusive property.** (1318)

PRAYER

O Jesus, eternal Truth, strengthen my feeble forces: ... have pity on my misery. (69)

Dear God, give me the strength to bear my crosses patiently and to offer up my sufferings in union with my Crucified Savior and His Mother, Our Lady of Sorrows.

IN TIMES OF SUFFERING

Only Jesus knows how burdensome and difficult it is to accomplish one's duties when the soul is so interiorly tortured, the physical powers so weakened and the mind darkened. In the silence of my heart I kept saying to myself, "O Christ, may delights, honor and glory be Yours, and suffering be mine. I will not lag one step behind as I follow You, though thorns wound my feet." (70)

FIFTH SUNDAY OF LENT

FAUSTINA: As I was praying before the Blessed Sacrament and greeting the five wounds of Jesus, at each salutation I felt a torrent of graces gushing into my soul, giving me a foretaste of heaven and absolute confidence in God's mercy. (1337)

JESUS: **If My death has not convinced you of My love, what will?** (580)

PRAYER

God filled my soul with the interior light of a deeper knowledge of Him as Supreme Goodness and Supreme Beauty. I came to know how very much God loves me. (16)

Dear God, give me the strength to bear my crosses patiently and to offer up my sufferings in union with my Crucified Savior and His Mother, Our Lady of Sorrows.

IN TIMES OF SUFFERING

JESUS: **O child, especially beloved by Me, apple of My eye, rest a moment near My Heart and taste of the love in which you will delight for all eternity.** (1489)

FIFTH MONDAY OF LENT

FAUSTINA: I began Holy Lent in the way that Jesus wanted me to, making myself totally dependent upon His holy will and accepting with love everything that he sends me. I cannot practice any greater mortifications, because I am so very weak. This long illness has sapped my strength completely. I am uniting myself with Jesus through suffering. When I meditate on His Painful Passion, my physical sufferings are lessened. (1625)

JESUS: **I have need of your sufferings to rescue souls (1612). There is but one price at which souls are bought, and that is suffering united to my suffering on the cross (324). You will join prayers, fasts, mortifications, labors, and all sufferings to My prayer, fasting, mortifications, labors and sufferings and then they will have power before My Father (531). Help me, My daughter, to save souls. Join your sufferings to My Passion and offer them to the heavenly Father for sinners. (1032)**

PRAYER

I abandon myself entirely to the action of Your grace. Let Your will be accomplished entirely in me, O Lord. (1326)

Dear God, give me the strength to bear my crosses patiently and to offer up my sufferings in union with my Crucified Savior and His Mother, Our Lady of Sorrows.

IN TIMES OF SUFFERING

I will daily repeat this act of self-oblation by pronouncing the following prayer which you Yourself have taught me, Jesus:

O Blood and Water which gushed forth from the Heart of Jesus as a Fount of Mercy for us, I trust in You! (309)

FIFTH TUESDAY OF LENT

FAUSTINA: The Lord gave me an occasion to practice patience through a particular person with whom I have to carry out a certain task. She is slower than anyone I have ever seen. One has to arm oneself with great patience to listen to her tedious talk (1376).... [T]he greatest power is hidden in patience. I see that patience always leads to victory, ... (1514) Before every major grace, my soul undergoes a test of patience, ... (1084)

JESUS: **Bear with yourself with great patience.** (1760)

PRAYER

O Jesus, my only solace! How frightful is this exile! How terrible this wilderness I have to cross! My soul is struggling through a terrible thicket of all kinds of difficulties. If You Yourself did not support me, Lord, there would be no thought of my moving forward. (1606)

Dear God, give me the strength to bear my crosses patiently and to offer up my sufferings in union with my Crucified Savior and His Mother, Our Lady of Sorrows.

IN TIMES OF SUFFERING

Let the soul be aware that, in order to pray and persevere in prayer, one must arm oneself with patience and cope bravely with exterior and interior difficulties. The interior difficulties are discouragement, dryness, heaviness of spirit and temptations. The exterior difficulties are human respect and time; one must observe the time set apart for prayer. (147)

A soul arms itself by prayer for all kinds of combat. In whatever state the soul may be, it ought to pray. A soul which is pure and beautiful must pray, or else it will lose its beauty; a soul which is striving after this purity must pray, or else it will never attain it; a soul which is newly converted must pray, or else it will fall again; a sinful soul, plunged in sins, must pray so that it might rise again. There is no soul which is not bound to pray, for every single grace comes to the soul through prayer (146).

FIFTH WEDNESDAY OF LENT

FAUSTINA: My heart is always open to the sufferings of others; and I will not close my heart to the sufferings of others, even though because of this I have been scornfully nicknamed "dump"; that is, [because] everyone dumps his pain into my heart. [To this] I answered that everyone has a place in my heart and I, in return, have a place in the Heart of Jesus. (871)

JESUS: ... I saw the Infant Jesus near my kneeler. He appeared to be about one year old, and He asked me to take Him in my arms.... It is good for Me to be close to your heart. "Although You are so little, I know that You are God. Why do You take the appearance of such a little baby to commune with me?" Because I want to teach you spiritual childhood. I want you to be very little, because when you are little, I carry you close to My Heart, just as you are holding Me close to your heart right now. (1481)

PRAYER

In difficult moments, I will fix my gaze upon the silent Heart of Jesus, stretched upon the Cross, and from the exploding flames of His merciful Heart, will flow down upon me power and strength to keep fighting. (906)

Dear God, give me the strength to bear my crosses patiently and to offer up my sufferings in union with my Crucified Savior and His Mother, Our Lady of Sorrows.

IN TIMES OF SUFFERING

JESUS: My daughter, I am told that there is much simplicity in you, so why do you not tell Me about everything that concerns you, even the smallest details? Tell Me about everything, and know that this will give

Me great joy. I answered, "But You know about everything, Lord." And Jesus replied to me, Yes, I do know; but you should not excuse yourself with the fact that I know, but with childlike simplicity talk to Me about everything, for My ears and heart are inclined towards you, and your words are dear to Me. (921)

FIFTH THURSDAY OF LENT

SOUL/FAUSTINA: Poor health detains me on the way to holiness. I cannot fulfill my duties. I am as useless as an extra wheel on a wagon. I cannot mortify myself or fast to any extent, as the saints did. Furthermore, nobody believes I am sick, so that mental pain is added to those of the body, and I am often humiliated. Jesus, how can anyone become holy in such circumstances? (1487)

JESUS: **True, my child, all that is painful. But there is no way to heaven except the way of the cross. I followed it first. You must learn that it is the shortest and surest way.** (1487)

PRAYER

O Living Host, support me in this exile, that I may be empowered to walk faithfully in the footsteps of the Savior. I do not ask, Lord, that You take me down from the cross, but I implore You to give me the strength to remain steadfast upon it. (1484)

Dear God, give me the strength to bear my crosses patiently and to offer up my sufferings in union with my Crucified Savior and His Mother, Our Lady of Sorrows.

IN TIMES OF SUFFERING

SOUL/FAUSTINA: Jesus, do not leave me alone in suffering. You know, Lord, how weak I am. I am an abyss of wretchedness, I am nothingness itself; so what will be so strange if You leave me alone and I fall? I am an infant, Lord, so I cannot get along by myself. However, beyond all abandonment I trust, and in spite of my own feeling I trust, and I am being completely transformed into trust — often in spite of what I feel. (1489)

FIFTH FRIDAY OF LENT

FAUSTINA: Humiliation is my daily food. I understand that the bride must herself share in everything that is the groom's; and so His cloak of mockery must cover me, too. At those times when I suffer much, I try to remain silent, as I do not trust my tongue which, at such moments, is inclined to talk for itself, while its duty is to help me praise God for all the blessings and gifts which He has given me. When I receive Jesus in Holy Communion, I ask Him fervently to deign to heal my tongue so that I would offend neither God nor neighbor by it. I want my tongue to praise God without cease. Great are the faults committed by the tongue. The soul will not attain sanctity if it does not keep watch over its tongue. (92)

JESUS: **Shun murmurs like a plague.** (1760)

PRAYER

All my strength is in You, O Living Bread. It would be difficult for me to live through the day if I did not receive Holy Communion. It is my shield; without You, Jesus, I know not how to live. (814)

Dear God, give me the strength to bear my crosses patiently and to offer up my sufferings in union with my Crucified Savior and His Mother, Our Lady of Sorrows.

IN TIMES OF SUFFERING

... I saw the suffering Savior. What struck me was that Jesus was so peaceful amidst His great sufferings. I understood that this was a lesson for me on what my outward behavior should be in the midst of my various sufferings. (1467)

FIFTH SATURDAY OF LENT

FAUSTINA: During the night, the Mother of God visited me, holding the Infant Jesus in Her arms. My soul was filled with joy, and I said, "Mary, my Mother, do You know how terribly I suffer?" And the Mother of

God answered me, *I know how much you suffer, but do not be afraid. I share with you your suffering, and I shall always do so.* She smiled warmly and disappeared. (25)

JESUS: **Ask my mother ... for help.** (1560)

PRAYER

O Mary, my sweet Mother,
To You I turn over my soul, my body and my poor heart.
Be the safeguard of my life,
Especially at death's hour, in the final fight. (161)

Dear God, give me the strength to bear my crosses patiently and to offer up my sufferings in union with my Crucified Savior and His Mother, Our Lady of Sorrows.

IN TIMES OF SUFFERING

O sweet Mother of God,
I model my life on You;
You are for me the bright dawn;
In You I lose myself, enraptured.

O Mother, Immaculate Virgin,
In You the divine ray is reflected,
Midst storms, 'tis You who teach me to love the Lord,
O my shield and defense from the foe. (1232)

MEDITATION BEFORE HOLY WEEK

FAUSTINA: If the angels were capable of envy, they would envy us for two things; one is the receiving of Holy Communion, and the other is suffering. (1804)

JESUS: ... **your suffering will become a source of your sanctification.** (1487)

PRAYER

O Blessed Host, in golden chalice enclosed for me,
That through the vast wilderness of exile
I may pass—pure, immaculate, undefiled;
Oh, grant that through the power of Your love
This might come to be.

O Blessed Host, take up Your dwelling within my soul,
O Thou my heart's purest love!
With Your brilliance the darkness dispel.
Refuse not Your grace to a humble heart.
O Blessed Host, enchantment of all heaven,

Though Your beauty be veiled
And captured in a crumb of bread,
Strong faith tears away that veil. (159)

Dear God, give me the strength to bear my crosses patiently and to offer up my sufferings in union with my Crucified Savior and His Mother, Our Lady of Sorrows.

IN TIMES OF SUFFERING

Oh, if only the suffering soul knew how it is loved by God, it would die of joy and excess of happiness! Someday, we will know the value of suffering, but then we will no longer be able to suffer. The present moment is ours. (963)

PALM SUNDAY

FAUSTINA: Palm Sunday. I attended Holy Mass, but did not have the strength to go and get the palm. I felt so weak that I barely made it till the end of Mass. During Mass, Jesus gave me to know the pain of His soul, and I could clearly feel how the hymns of Hosanna reverberated as a painful echo in His Sacred Heart. My soul, too, was inundated by a sea of bitterness, and each Hosanna pierced my own heart to its depths. My whole soul was drawn close to Jesus. (1657)

JESUS: **My daughter, your compassion for Me refreshes Me. By meditating on My Passion, your soul acquires a distinct beauty.** (1657)

PRAYER

I am prepared for all sacrifices for Your sake, but You know that I am weakness itself. Nevertheless, with You I can do all things. O my Jesus, I beseech You, be with me at each instant. (954)

Dear God, give me the strength to bear my crosses patiently and to offer up my sufferings in union with my Crucified Savior and His Mother, Our Lady of Sorrows.

IN TIMES OF SUFFERING

My Jesus, support me when difficult and stormy days come, days of testing, days of ordeal, when suffering and fatigue begin to oppress my body and my soul. Sustain me, Jesus, and give me strength to bear suffering. Set a guard upon my lips that they may address no word of complaint to creatures. Your most merciful Heart is all my hope. I have nothing for my defense but only Your mercy; in it lies all my trust. (1065)

MONDAY OF HOLY WEEK

FAUSTINA: Jesus, when I look at Your suffering, I see that I am doing next to nothing for the salvation of souls. (1184)

JESUS: **Know, My daughter, that your silent day-to-day martyrdom in complete submission to My will ushers many souls into heaven. And when it seems to you that your suffering exceeds your strength,**

contemplate My wounds, and you will rise above human scorn and judgment. Meditation on My passion will help you rise above all things. (1184)

PRAYER

My Jesus, I now see that I have gone through all the stages of my life following You: childhood, youth, vocation, apostolic work, Tabor, Gethsemane, and now I am already with You on Calvary (1580). For the sake of His sorrowful Passion, show us Your mercy, that we may praise the omnipotence of Your mercy forever and ever. Amen. (1211).

Dear God, give me the strength to bear my crosses patiently and to offer up my sufferings in union with my Crucified Savior and His Mother, Our Lady of Sorrows.

IN TIMES OF SUFFERING

O Jesus, what darkness is enveloping me and what nothingness is penetrating me. But, my Jesus, do not leave me alone; grant me the grace of faithfulness. Although I cannot penetrate the mystery of God's visitation, it is in my power to say: Your will be done. (1237)

I will glorify You in abandonment and darkness, in agony and fear, in pain and bitterness, in anguish of spirit and grief of heart. In all things may You be blessed. (1662)

TUESDAY OF HOLY WEEK

FAUSTINA: This evening, one of the deceased sisters came and asked me for one day of fasting and to offer all my [spiritual] exercises on that day for her. I answered that I would. (1185)

From early morning on the following day, I offered everything for her intention. During Holy Mass, I had a brief experience of her torment. I experienced such intense hunger for God that I seemed to be dying of the desire to become united with Him. This lasted only a short time, but I understood what the longing of the souls in purgatory was like. (1186)

JESUS: **Enter into purgatory often, because they need you there.** (1738)

PRAYER

In the meditation on death, I prepared myself as if for real death. I examined my conscience and searched all my affairs at the approach of death and, thanks be to grace, my affairs were directed toward that ultimate goal. This filled my heart with great gratitude to God, and I resolved to serve my God even more faithfully in the future. One thing alone is necessary: to put my old self to death and to begin a new life. In the morning, I prepared to receive Holy Communion as if it were to be the last in my life, and after Holy Communion I brought before my imagination my actual death, and I said the prayers for the dying and then the *De Profundis* for my own soul. (1343)

Dear God, give me the strength to bear my crosses patiently and to offer up my sufferings in union with my Crucified Savior and His Mother, Our Lady of Sorrows.

IN TIMES OF SUFFERING

I plead with You for the souls that are most in need of prayer. I plead for the dying; be merciful to them. I also beg You, Jesus, to free all souls from purgatory. (240)

PSALM 130

Out of the depths I cry to thee O Lord!
Lord, hear my voice!
Let thy ears be attentive
To the voice of my supplications!

If thou, O Lord, should mark iniquities,
Lord, who could stand?
But there is forgiveness with thee,
that thou mayest be feared.

I wait for the Lord, my soul waits,
And in his work I hope;
my soul waits for the Lord
more than watchmen for the morning,
more than watchmen for the morning.

O Israel, hope in the Lord!
For with the Lord there is steadfast love,
and with him is plenteous redemption.

And he will redeem Israel
From all his iniquities.

WEDNESDAY OF HOLY WEEK

FAUSTINA: O my Jesus, my Master, I unite my desires to the desires that You had on the cross: I desire to fulfill Your holy will; I desire the conversion of souls; I desire that Your mercy be adored; I desire that the triumph of the Church be hastened; ... (1581)

JESUS: **Look, and enter into My Passion.** (1663)

PRAYER

... it is You, Jesus, stretched out on the Cross who give me strength and are always close to the suffering soul. (1508)

Dear God, give me the strength to bear my crosses patiently and to offer up my sufferings in union with my Crucified Savior and His Mother, Our Lady of Sorrows.

IN TIMES OF SUFFERING

O my Jesus, despite the deep night that is all around me and the dark clouds which hide the horizon, I know that the sun never goes out. O Lord, though I cannot comprehend You and do not understand Your ways, I nonetheless trust in Your mercy. If it is Your will, Lord, that I live always in such darkness, may You be blessed. I ask You only one thing, Jesus: do not allow me to offend You in any way. O my Jesus, You alone know the longings and the sufferings of my heart. I am glad I can suffer for You, however little. When I feel that the suffering is more than I can bear, I take refuge in the Lord in the Blessed Sacrament, and I speak to Him with profound silence. (73)

HOLY THURSDAY

FAUSTINA: The courage and strength that are in me are not of me, but of Him who lives in me — it is the Eucharist. (91)

The Lord's Supper is laid,
Jesus sits down at table with His Apostles,
His Being all transformed into love,
For such was the Holy Trinity's counsel.

With great desire, I desire to eat with you,
Before I suffer death.
About to leave you, love holds Me in your midst.
He sheds His Blood, gives His life, for He loves immensely.

Love hides beneath the appearance of bread,
Departing, He remains with us.
Such self-abasement was not needed,
Yet burning love hid Him under these species.

Over the bread and wine He says these words:
"This is My Blood, this is My Body."
Although mysterious, these are words of love.
Then He passes the Cup among His disciples.

Jesus grew deeply troubled within
And said, "One of you will betray his Master."
They fell silent, with a silence as of the tomb,
And John inclined his head on His breast.

The supper is ended.
Let us go to Gethsemane.
Love is satisfied,
And there the traitor is waiting. (1002)

JESUS: **In the Host is your power; it will defend you (616). But I want to tell you that eternal life must begin already here on earth through Holy Communion. Each Holy Communion makes you more capable of communing with God throughout eternity. (1811)**

PRAYER

Jesus concealed in the Host is everything to me. From the tabernacle I draw strength, power, courage and light. Here, I seek consolation in time of anguish. (1037)

I am never alone, because He is my constant companion. He is present to me at every moment. (318)

Dear God, give me the strength to bear my crosses patiently and to offer up my sufferings in union with my Crucified Savior and His Mother, Our Lady of Sorrows.

IN TIMES OF SUFFERING

During the Holy Hour, the Lord allowed me to taste His Passion. I shared in the bitterness of the suffering that filled His soul to overflowing. Jesus gave me to understand how a soul should be faithful to prayer despite torments, dryness, and temptations; because oftentimes the realization of God's great plans depends mainly on such prayer. If we do not persevere in such prayer, we frustrate what the Lord wanted to do through us or within us. Let every soul remember these words: "And being in anguish, He prayed longer." (872)

Once while saying the Rosary, St. Faustina suddenly saw a ciborium with the Blessed Sacrament, uncovered and full of hosts. She heard a voice from the ciborium saying: **"These hosts have been received by souls converted through your prayer and suffering."** (709)

Before the vigil supper, I entered the chapel for a moment to break the wafer spiritually with those dear to my heart. I presented them all, by name, to Jesus and begged for graces on their behalf. But that wasn't all. I commended to the Lord all those who are being persecuted, those who are suffering, those who do not know His Name, and especially poor sinners. (845)

O BLESSED HOST LITANY

O Blessed Host, in whom is contained the testament of God's mercy for us, and especially for poor sinners.

O Blessed Host, in whom is contained the Body and Blood of the Lord Jesus as proof of infinite mercy for us, and especially for poor sinners.

O Blessed Host, in whom is contained life eternal and of infinite mercy, dispensed in abundance to us and especially to poor sinners.

O Blessed Host, in whom is contained the mercy of the Father, the Son, and the Holy Spirit toward us, and especially toward poor sinners.

O Blessed Host, in whom is contained the infinite price of mercy which will compensate for all our debts, and especially those of poor sinners.

O Blessed Host, in whom is contained the fountain of living water which springs from infinite mercy for us, and especially for poor sinners.

O Blessed Host, in whom is contained the fire of purest love which blazes forth from the bosom of the Eternal Father, as from an abyss of infinite mercy for us, and especially for poor sinners.

O Blessed Host, in whom is contained the medicine for all our infirmities, flowing from infinite mercy, as from a fount, for us and especially for poor sinners.

O Blessed Host, in whom is contained the union between God and us through His infinite mercy for us, and especially for poor sinners.

O Blessed Host, in whom are contained all the sentiments of the most sweet Heart of Jesus toward us, and especially poor sinners. (356)

GOOD FRIDAY

FAUSTINA: O Mary, today a terrible sword has pierced your holy soul. Except for God, no one knows of your suffering. Your soul does not break; it is brave, because it is with Jesus. (915)

JESUS: **At three o'clock, implore My mercy, especially for sinners; and, if only for a brief moment, immerse yourself in My Passion, particularly in My abandonment at the moment of agony. This is the hour of great mercy for the whole world. I will allow you to enter into My mortal sorrow. In this hour, I will refuse nothing to the soul that makes a request of me in virtue of My Passion.** (1320)

PRAYER

Jesus, I beg You, by the inconceivable power of Your mercy, that all the souls who will die today escape the fire of hell, even if they have been the greatest sinners. Today is Friday, the memorial of Your bitter agony on the Cross; because Your mercy is inconceivable, the Angels will not be surprised at this. (873)

Dear God, give me the strength to bear my crosses patiently and to offer up my sufferings in union with my Crucified Savior and His Mother, Our Lady of Sorrows.

IN TIMES OF SUFFERING

PRAYER TO JESUS CRUCIFIED

When pain overwhelms my soul,
And the horizon darkens like night,
And the heart is torn with the torment of suffering,
Jesus Crucified, You are my strength.

When the soul, dimmed with pain,
Exerts itself in battle without respite,
And the heart is in agony and torment,
Jesus Crucified, You are the hope of my salvation.

And so the days pass,
As the soul bathes in a sea of bitterness,
And the heart dissolves in tears,
Jesus Crucified, You shine for me like the dawn.

And when the cup of bitterness brims over,
And all things conspire against her,
And the soul goes down to the Garden of Olives,
Jesus Crucified, in You is my defense.

When the soul, conscious of its innocence,
Accepts these dispensations from God,
The heart can then repay hurts with love.
Jesus Crucified, transform my weakness into omnipotence. (1151)

(Today begin the Novena and Divine Mercy Chaplet. See page 159.)

HOLY SATURDAY

FAUSTINA: A silent soul is strong; no adversities will harm it if it perseveres in silence. The silent soul is capable of attaining the closest union with God. It lives almost always under the inspiration of the Holy Spirit. God works in a silent soul without hindrance. (477)

JESUS: **Strive for a life of recollection so that you can hear My voice, which is so soft that only recollected souls can hear it.** (1779)

PRAYER

My particular examen is still the same; namely union with the merciful Christ, and silence. The flower which I lay at the feet of the Mother of God ... is my practice of silence. (1105)

O Mary, my Mother and my Lady, I offer you my soul, my body, my life and my death, and all that will follow it. I place everything in your hands. (79)

> O Mary, Immaculate Virgin,
> Pure crystal for my heart,
> You are my strength, O secure anchor,
> You are a shield and protection for a weak heart. (161)

Dear God, give me the strength to bear my crosses patiently and to offer up my sufferings in union with my Crucified Savior and His Mother, Our Lady of Sorrows.

Then I saw the Blessed Virgin, unspeakably beautiful. She came down from the altar to my kneeler, held me close to herself and said to me, *I am Mother to you all, thanks to the unfathomable mercy of God. Most pleasing to Me is that soul which faithfully carries out the will of God.* She gave me to understand that I had faithfully fulfilled the will of God and had thus found favor in His eyes. *Be courageous. Do not fear apparent obstacles, but fix your gaze upon the Passion of My Son, and in this way you will be victorious.* (449)

EASTER SUNDAY

FAUSTINA: Hail, most merciful Heart of Jesus,
    Living Fountain of all graces,
    Our sole shelter, our only refuge;
    In You I have the light of hope.

    Hail, most compassionate Heart of my God,
    Unfathomable living Fount of Love
    From which gushes life for sinful man
    And the Spring of all sweetness.

    Hail, open Wound of the Most Sacred Heart,
    From which the rays of mercy issued forth
    And from which it was given us to draw life
    With the vessel of trust alone.

Hail, God's goodness, incomprehensible,
Never to be measured or fathomed,
Full of love and mercy, though always holy,
Yet, like a good mother, ever bent o'er us.

Hail, Throne of Mercy, Lamb of God,
Who gave Your life in sacrifice for me,
Before whom my soul humbles itself daily,
Living in faith profound. (1321)

JESUS: ... I too came down from heaven out of love for you; I lived for you, I died for you, and I created the heavens for you. (853)

PRAYER

Jesus, Supreme Light, grant me the grace of knowing myself, and pierce my dark soul with Your light, and fill the abyss of my soul with Your own self,... (297)

Dear God, give me the strength to bear my crosses patiently and to offer up my sufferings in union with my Crucified Savior and His Mother, Our Lady of Sorrows.

IN TIMES OF SUFFERING

O Supreme Good, I want to love You as no one on earth has ever loved You before! I want to adore You with every moment of my life and unite my will closely to Your holy will. My life is not drab or monotonous, but it is varied like a garden of fragrant flowers, so that I don't know which flower to pick first, the lily of suffering or the rose of love of neighbor or the violet of humility. I will not enumerate these treasures in which my every day abounds. It is a great thing to know how to make use of the present moment. (296)

EASTER MONDAY

FAUSTINA: ... I saw the Lord Jesus in the midst of a great light. He approached me and said, **Peace be to you, My children**, and He lifted up His hand and gave His blessing. The wounds in His hands, feet and side were indelible and shining. When he looked at me with such kindness and love, my whole soul drowned itself in Him.

JESUS: **You have taken a great part in My Passion; therefore I now give you a great share in My joy and glory.** The whole time of the Resurrection [Mass] seemed like only a minute to me. A wondrous recollection filled my soul and lasted throughout the whole festal season. The kindness of Jesus is so great that I cannot express it. (205)

PRAYER

O my Jesus, my only hope, thank You for the book which You have opened before my soul's eyes. That book is Your Passion which You underwent for love of me. It is from this book that I have learned how to love God and souls. (304)

Dear God, give me the strength to bear my crosses patiently and to offer up my sufferings in union with my Crucified Savior and His Mother, Our Lady of Sorrows.

IN TIMES OF SUFFERING

... give me death when, humanly speaking, my life seems particularly necessary, be blessed. Should You take me in my youth, be blessed; should You let me live to a ripe old age, be blessed. Should You give me health and strength, be blessed; should you confine me to a bed of pain for my whole life, be blessed. Should you give only failures and disappointments in life, be blessed. Should You allow my purest intentions to be condemned, be blessed. Should You enlighten my mind, be blessed. Should You leave me in darkness and all kinds of torments, be blessed.

From this moment on, I live in the deepest peace, because the Lord Himself is carrying me in the hollow of His hand. He, Lord of unfathomable mercy, knows that I desire Him alone in all things, always and everywhere. (1264)

EASTER TUESDAY

FAUSTINA: I prayed today for a soul in agony, who was dying without the Holy Sacraments, although she desired them. But it was already too late. It was a relative of mine, my uncle's wife. She was a soul pleasing to God. There was no distance between us at that moment. (207]

JESUS: Write that when they say this chaplet in the presence of the dying, I will stand between My Father and the dying person, not as the just Judge but as the merciful Savior ... and the hour of their death will be a happy one. (1541)

PRAYER

I realize more and more how much every soul needs God's mercy throughout life and particularly at the hour of death. This chaplet mitigates God's anger, as He Himself told me (1036). **"This prayer will serve to appease My wrath."** (476)

Oh, dying souls are in such great need of prayer! O Jesus, inspire souls to pray often for the dying. (1015)

O my Jesus, Life of my soul, my Life, my Savior, my sweetest Bridegroom, and at the same time my Judge, You know that in this last hour of mine I do not count on any merits of my own, but only on Your mercy. Even as of today, I immerse myself totally in the abyss of Your mercy, which is always open to every soul. (1553)

Dear God, give me the strength to bear my crosses patiently and to offer up my sufferings in union with my Crucified Savior and His Mother, Our Lady of Sorrows.

IN TIMES OF SUFFERING

God's mercy sometimes touches the sinner even at the last moment, in a wondrous and mysterious way. Outwardly, it seems as if everything is lost, but it is not so. The soul, illumined by a ray of God's powerful final grace, turns to God in the last moment, with such a power of love that in an instant, it receives from God, forgiveness of all sin and punishment, while outwardly it shows no sign either of repentance or of contrition, because souls [at that stage] no longer react to external things. (1698)

When I immersed myself in prayer and united myself with all the Masses that were being celebrated all over the world at that time, I implored God, for the sake of all these Holy Masses, to have mercy on the world and especially on poor sinners who were dying at that moment. At the same instant, I received an interior answer from God that a thousand souls had received grace through the prayerful mediation I had offered to God. We do not know the number of souls that is ours to save through our prayers and sacrifices; therefore, let us always pray for sinners. (1783)

EASTER WEDNESDAY

FAUSTINA: Oh, if souls would only be willing to listen, at least a little, to the voice of conscience and the voice — that is, the inspirations — of the Holy Spirit! I say "at least a little," because once we open ourselves to the influence of the Holy Spirit, He Himself will fulfill what is lacking in us. (359)

JESUS: **Host pleasing to My Father, know, My daughter, that the entire Holy Trinity finds Its special delight in you, because you live exclusively by the will of God. No sacrifice can compare with this.** (955)

PRAYER

O Jesus, keep me in holy fear, so that I may not waste graces. Help me to be faithful to the inspirations of the Holy Spirit. Grant that my heart may burst for love of You, rather than I should neglect even one act of love for You. (1557)

Dear God, give me the strength to bear my crosses patiently and to offer up my sufferings in union with my Crucified Savior and His Mother, Our Lady of Sorrows.

IN TIMES OF SUFFERING

O Divine Spirit, Spirit of truth and of light,
Dwell ever in my soul by Your divine grace.
May Your breath dissipate the darkness,
And in this light may good deeds be multiplied.

O divine Spirit, Spirit of love and of mercy,
You pour the balm of trust into my heart,
Your grace confirms my soul in good,
Giving it the invincible power of constancy.

O Divine Spirit, Spirit of peace and of joy,
You invigorate my thirsting heart
And pour into it the living fountain of God's love,
Making it intrepid for battle.

O Divine Spirit, my soul's most welcome guest,
For my part, I want to remain faithful to You;
Both in days of joy and in the agony of suffering,
I want always, O Spirit of God, to live in Your presence.

O Divine Spirit, who pervade my whole being
And give me to know Your Divine, Triune Life,
And lead me into the mystery of Your Divine Being,
Initiating me into Your Divine Essence,
Thus united to You, I will live a life without end. (1411)

EASTER THURSDAY

FAUSTINA: I have learned that the greatest power is hidden in patience. I see that patience always leads to victory, although not immediately; but that victory will become manifest after many years. (1514)

JESUS: **My daughter, have patience; ...** (858)

PRAYER

I am going forward through life amidst rainbows and storms, but with my head held high with pride, for I am a royal child. I feel that the blood of Jesus is circulating in my veins, and I have put my trust in the great mercy of the Lord. (992)

Dear God, give me the strength to bear my crosses patiently and to offer up my sufferings in union with my Crucified Savior and His Mother, Our Lady of Sorrows.

I see that the will of God has not yet been fulfilled in me, and that is why I must live, for I know that if I fulfill everything the Lord has planned for me in this world, He will not leave me in exile any longer, for heaven is my home. But before we go to our Homeland, we must fulfill the will of God on earth; that is, trials and struggles must run their full course in us. (897)

EASTER FRIDAY

FAUSTINA: Thank You, O Lord, for creating me,
  For calling me into being from nothingness,
  For imprinting Your divinity on my soul,
  The work of sheer merciful love. (1286)

JESUS: **Before I made the world, I loved you with the love your heart is experiencing today, and throughout the centuries, My love will never change.** (1754)

PRAYER

What a paradise it is for a soul when the heart knows itself to be so loved by God.... (1756)

... the Lord gave me an understanding of God's incomprehensible love for people. He lifts us up to His very Godhead. His only motives are love and fathomless mercy. (1172)

You have surrounded my life with Your tender and loving care, more than I can comprehend, for I will understand Your goodness in its entirety only when the veil is lifted. I desire that my whole life be but one act of thanksgiving to You, O God. (1285)

Dear God, give me the strength to bear my crosses patiently and to offer up my sufferings in union with my Crucified Savior and His Mother, Our Lady of Sorrows.

IN TIMES OF SUFFERING

O Jesus, I want to live in the present moment, to live as if this were the last day of my life. I want to use every moment scrupulously for the greater glory of God, to use every circumstance for the benefit of my soul. I want to look upon everything from the point of view that nothing happens without the will of God. God of unfathomable mercy, embrace the whole world and pour Yourself out upon us through the merciful Heart of Jesus. (1183)

EASTER SATURDAY

FAUSTINA: When I had rested near His sweetest Heart, I told Him, "Jesus, I have so much to tell You." And the Lord said to me with great love, **Speak, My daughter.** And I started to enumerate the pains of my heart; that is, how greatly concerned I am for all mankind, that "they all do not know You, and those who do know You do not love You as

You deserve to be loved. I also see how terribly sinners offend You; and then again, I see how severely the faithful, especially Your servants, are oppressed and persecuted. And then, too, I see many souls rushing headlong into the terrible abyss of hell. You see, Jesus, this is the pain that gnaws at my heart and bones. And, although You show me special love and inundate my heart with streams of Your joys, nevertheless, this does not appease the sufferings I have just mentioned, but rather they penetrate my poor heart all the more acutely. Oh, how ardently I desire that all mankind turn with trust to Your mercy. Then, seeing the glory of Your name, my heart will be comforted."

JESUS: **My daughter, those words of your heart are pleasing to Me, and by saying the chaplet you are bringing humankind closer to Me.** (929)

PRAYER

O Wound of Mercy, Heart of Jesus, hide me in Your depths as a drop of Your own blood, and do not let me out forever! Lock me in Your depths, and do You Yourself teach me to love You! Eternal Love, do You Yourself form my soul that it be made capable of returning Your love. (1631)

Dear God, give me the strength to bear my crosses patiently and to offer up my sufferings in union with my Crucified Savior and His Mother, Our Lady of Sorrows.

IN TIMES OF SUFFERING

I remind you, My daughter, that as often as you hear the clock strike the third hour, immerse yourself completely in My mercy, adoring and glorifying it; invoke its omnipotence for the whole world, and

particularly for poor sinners; for at that moment mercy was opened wide for every soul ... it was the hour of grace for the whole world—mercy triumphed over justice. (1572)

Through the chaplet you will obtain everything, if what you ask for is compatible with My will. (1731)

DIVINE MERCY SUNDAY

FAUSTINA: O Jesus, I understand that Your mercy is beyond all imagining, and therefore I ask You to make my heart so big that there will be room in it for the needs of all the souls living on the face of the earth. O Jesus, my love extends beyond the world, to the souls suffering in purgatory, and I want to exercise mercy toward them by means of indulgenced prayers. God's mercy is unfathomable and inexhaustible, just as God Himself is unfathomable. Even if I were to use the strongest words there are to express this mercy of God, all this would be nothing in comparison with what it is in reality. O Jesus, make my heart sensitive to all the sufferings of my neighbor, whether of body or of soul. O my Jesus, I know that You act toward us as we act toward our neighbor. (692)

JESUS: From all My wounds, like from streams, mercy flows for souls, but the wound in My Heart is the fountain of unfathomable mercy. From this fountain spring all graces for souls. The flames of compassion burn Me. I desire greatly to pour them out upon souls. Speak to the whole world about My mercy. (1190)

PRAYER

Jesus, I Trust in You! (1209)

Dear God, give me the strength to bear my crosses patiently and to offer up my sufferings in union with my Crucified Savior and His Mother, Our Lady of Sorrows.

IN TIMES OF SUFFERING

All things will have an end in this vale of tears,
Tears will run dry and pain will cease.
Only one thing will remain—
Love for You, O Lord.

All things will have an end in this exile,
The ordeals and wilderness of the soul.
And though she live in perpetual agony,
If God is with her, nothing can shake her. (1132)

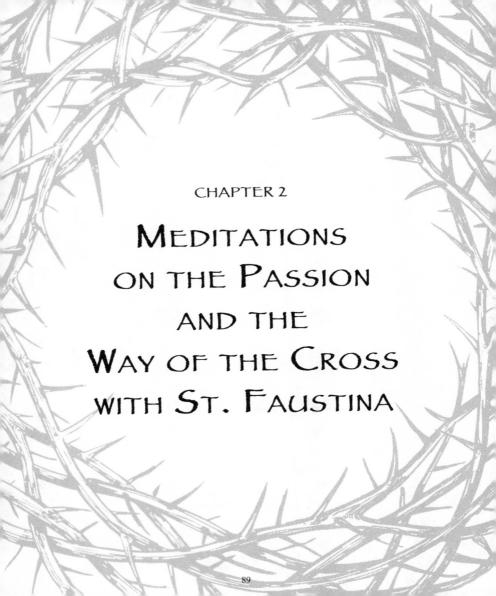

CHAPTER 2

MEDITATIONS ON THE PASSION AND THE WAY OF THE CROSS WITH ST. FAUSTINA

Almighty Father, I place the Precious Blood of Jesus before my lips before I pray, that my prayers may be purified before they ascend to Your divine altar. — St. Mary Magdalen dei Pazzi

FAUSTINA: He who wants to learn humility should reflect upon the Passion of Jesus. (267)

JESUS TO ST. FAUSTINA: **There are few souls who contemplate My Passion with true feeling; I give great graces to souls who meditate devoutly on my Passion.** (737)

MEDITATION
HOLY THURSDAY: THE INSTITUTION OF THE EUCHARIST

During this hour of prayer, Jesus allowed me to enter the Cenacle, and I was a witness to what happened there. However, I was most deeply moved when, before the Consecration, Jesus raised His eyes to heaven and entered into a mysterious conversation with His Father. It is only in eternity that we shall really understand that moment. His eyes were like two flames; His face was radiant, white as snow; His whole personage full of majesty, His soul full of longing. At the moment of Consecration, love rested satiated—the sacrifice fully consummated.... Oh, how ardently

I desire that the whole world would come to know this unfathomable mystery. (684)

O great Passion! O deep Wounds! O blood shed in abundance! O God of meekness, O cruel death, have mercy on me.

MEDITATION
JESUS ENTERS HIS PASSION

Jesus gave me to know of the sufferings He experienced there. The world will learn about them on the day of judgment (1515). My soul was filled with pain and longing; in my soul, I felt great hatred for sin, and even the smallest infidelity on my part seemed to me like a huge mountain for which I must expiate my mortification and penance. (948)

Let every soul remember these words: *"And being in anguish, He prayed longer."* I always prolong such prayer as much as is in my power. (872)

O Divine Will, You are the delight of my heart, the food of my soul, the light of my intellect, the omnipotent strength of my will; for when I unite myself with Your will, O Lord, Your power works through me and takes the place of my feeble will. Each day, I seek to carry out God's wishes. (650)

O great Passion! O deep Wounds! O blood shed in abundance! O God of meekness, O cruel death, have mercy on me.

MEDITATION
JESUS PROSTRATE IN THE GARDEN

... I took part in His Agony in the Garden, ... (1276). From my breast there escaped one continuous moan. A natural dying will be much easier because then one is in agony and will die; while here, one is in agony, but cannot die. O Jesus, I never thought such suffering could exist. Nothingness: that is the reality. O Jesus, Save me! (1558)

PRAYER

O great Passion! O deep Wounds! O blood shed in abundance! O God of meekness, O cruel death, have mercy on me.

FIRST STATION
JESUS IS CONDEMNED BY PILATE

JESUS: Consider My sufferings before Pilate.

I meditated upon His sorrowful Passion for one week.... The superiors were indeed very solicitous for the sick, but the Lord ordained that I should feel forsaken. This best of masters withdraws every created thing in order that He Himself might act. (149)

O great Passion! O deep Wounds! O blood shed in abundance! O God of meekness, O cruel death, have mercy on me.

MEDITATION
JESUS IS SCOURGED AT THE PILLAR

I saw how the Lord Jesus suffered as He was being scourged. Oh, such an inconceivable agony!

The Lord said to me I suffer even greater suffering than that which you see (188). And Jesus gave me to know for what sins He subjected himself to the scourging; these are sins of impurity (445). O poor sinners, on the day of judgment how will you face the Jesus whom you are now torturing so cruelly. His blood flowed to the ground, and in some places His flesh started to fall off. I saw a few bare bones on His back. The meek Jesus moaned softly and sighed. (188)

PRAYER

O great Passion! O deep Wounds! O blood shed in abundance! O God of meekness, O cruel death, have mercy on me.

MEDITATION
JESUS IS CROWNED WITH THORNS

And they wove a crown of thorns, which they put on His sacred head. They put a reed in His hand and made fun of Him, ... Some spat in His face, while others took the reed and struck Him on the head with it. Others caused him pain by slapping Him; still others covered His face and struck Him with their fists. Jesus bore all this with meekness (408). Patience is linked to meekness. (1514)

Who can comprehend Him — comprehend His suffering? Jesus' eyes were downcast. I sensed what was happening in the most sweet Heart of Jesus at that time. Let every soul reflect on what Jesus was suffering at that moment. (408)

PRAYER

O great Passion! O deep Wounds! O blood shed in abundance! O God of meekness, O cruel death, have mercy on me.

SECOND STATION
JESUS BEARS HIS CROSS

True love of God consists in carrying out God's will. To show God our love in what we do, all our actions, even the least, must spring out of love of God (279). The moment I knelt down to cross out my own will,... I heard this voice in my soul: **"From today on, do not fear God's judgment, for you will not be judged."** (374)

PRAYER

O great Passion! O deep Wounds! O blood shed in abundance! O God of meekness, O cruel death, have mercy on me.

THIRD STATION
JESUS FALLS THE FIRST TIME

My Jesus, despite Your graces, I see and feel all my misery. I begin my day with battle and end it with battle. As soon as I conquer one obstacle, ten more appear to take its place. But I am not worried, because I know that this is the time of struggle, not peace. When the burden of the battle becomes too much for me, I throw myself like a child into the arms of the heavenly Father and trust I will not perish. O my Jesus, how prone I am to evil, and this forces me to be constantly vigilant. But I do not lose heart. I trust God's grace, which abounds in the worst misery. (606)

PRAYER

O great Passion! O deep Wounds! O blood shed in abundance! O God of meekness, O cruel death, have mercy on me.

FOURTH STATION
JESUS MEETS HIS BLESSED MOTHER

Mother of God, your soul was plunged into a sea of bitterness; look upon Your child and teach her to suffer and to love while suffering. Fortify my soul that pain will not break it. Mother of Grace, teach me to live [by the power of] God. (315)

PRAYER

O great Passion! O deep Wounds! O blood shed in abundance! O God of meekness, O cruel death, have mercy on me.

FIFTH STATION
SIMON OF CYRENE HELPS JESUS CARRY HIS CROSS

… Jesus, You do not give a reward for the successful performance of a work, but for the good will and the labor undertaken (952). I am learning how to be good from Jesus, from Him who is goodness itself, so I might be called a daughter of the heavenly Father. (669)

PRAYER

O great Passion! O deep Wounds! O blood shed in abundance! O God of meekness, O cruel death, have mercy on me.

SIXTH STATION
VERONICA WIPES THE FACE OF JESUS

I want to resemble You, O Jesus, — You crucified, tortured, and humiliated. Jesus, imprint upon my heart and soul Your own humility. I love You, Jesus, to the point of madness, You who were crushed with suffering as described by the prophet [cf. Isaiah 53:2–9], as if he could not see the human form in You because of Your great suffering. It is in this condition, Jesus, that I love you to the point of madness. O eternal and infinite God, what has love done to you? (267)

PRAYER

O great Passion! O deep Wounds! O blood shed in abundance! O God of meekness, O cruel death, have mercy on me.

SEVENTH STATION
JESUS FALLS THE SECOND TIME

O my Jesus, keep me near to You! See how weak I am! I cannot go a step forward by myself; so You, Jesus, must stand by me constantly like a mother by a helpless child—and even more so. (264)

PRAYER

O great Passion! O deep Wounds! O blood shed in abundance! O God of meekness, O cruel death, have mercy on me.

EIGHTH STATION
JESUS CONSOLES THE WOMEN OF JERUSALEM

O Jesus, if only I could become like mist before Your eyes, to cover the earth so that You would not see its terrible crimes. Jesus, when I look at the world and its indifference towards You, again and again it brings tears to my eyes;... (284). O Jesus, make my heart sensitive to all the sufferings of my neighbor, whether of body or soul. O my Jesus, I know that You act toward us as we act toward our neighbor. (692)

PRAYER

O great Passion! O deep Wounds! O blood shed in abundance! O God of meekness, O cruel death, have mercy on me.

NINTH STATION
JESUS FALLS THE THIRD TIME

In the midst of the worst difficulties and adversities, I do not lose inner peace or exterior balance, and this discourages my adversaries. Patience in adversity gives power to the soul. (607)

PRAYER

O great Passion! O deep Wounds! O blood shed in abundance! O God of meekness, O cruel death, have mercy on me.

TENTH STATION
JESUS IS STRIPPED OF HIS GARMENTS

Jesus was suddenly standing before me, stripped of His clothes, His body completely covered with wounds, His eyes flooded with tears and blood, His face disfigured and covered with spittle. (268)

Jesus said nothing, but just looked at me, and in that gaze I felt His pain, so terrible that we have not the faintest idea of how much He suffered for us before He was crucified.... When I see Jesus tormented, my heart is torn to pieces, and I think: what will become of sinners if they do not take advantage of the Passion of Jesus: In His Passion, I see a whole sea of mercy. (948)

O great Passion! O deep Wounds! O blood shed in abundance! O God of meekness, O cruel death, have mercy on me.

ELEVENTH STATION
JESUS IS NAILED TO THE CROSS

... I saw Jesus nailed to the Cross in such a way when God wanted to look at the earth, He had to look through the wounds of Jesus. And I understood that it was for the sake of Jesus that God blesses the earth. (60)

PRAYER

O great Passion! O deep Wounds! O blood shed in abundance! O God of meekness, O cruel death, have mercy on me.

MEDITATION
"I THIRST"

Good Friday. I saw the Lord Jesus, crucified, who looked at me and said, **I thirst** (648). **My daughter, help Me to save souls. You will go to a**

dying sinner, and you will continue to recite the chaplet, and in this way you will obtain for him trust in My mercy, for he is already in despair. (1797)

PRAYER

O great Passion! O deep Wounds! O blood shed in abundance! O God of meekness, O cruel death, have mercy on me.

TWELFTH STATION
JESUS DIES ON THE CROSS

... I saw the Lord Jesus just as He was during His Passion. His eyes were raised up to His Father, and He was praying for us (736). He who knows how to forgive prepares for himself many graces from God. As often as I look upon the cross, so often, will I forgive with all my heart. (390)

PRAYER

O great Passion! O deep Wounds! O blood shed in abundance! O God of meekness, O cruel death, have mercy on me.

THIRTEENTH STATION
JESUS IS PIERCED AND TAKEN DOWN FROM THE CROSS

You expired, Jesus, but the source of life gushed forth for souls, and the ocean of mercy opened up for the whole world (1319). From that Fount of Mercy issued the two rays, that is, the Blood and the Water.... In this open wound of the Heart of Jesus I enclose all poor humans ... and those individuals whom I love, ... (1309)

PRAYER

O great Passion! O deep Wounds! O blood shed in abundance! O God of meekness, O cruel death, have mercy on me.

FOURTEENTH STATION
JESUS IS LAID IN THE TOMB

I was reflecting on how much God has suffered and on how great was the love He had shown for us, and on the fact that we still do not believe that God loves us so much. O Jesus, who can understand this? What suffering it is for our Savior! How can He convince us of His love if even His death cannot convince us? (319)

O great Passion! O deep Wounds! O blood shed in abundance! O God of meekness, O cruel death, have mercy on me.

FIFTEENTH STATION
JESUS RISES FROM THE DEAD

Today, during the [Mass of the] Resurrection, I saw the Lord Jesus in the midst of a great light.... The wounds in His hands, feet and side were indelible and shining.... And He said to me, **You have taken a great part in my Passion; therefore, I now give you a great share in My joy and glory** (205). During Mass, I thanked the Lord Jesus for having deigned to redeem us and for having given us that greatest of all gifts; namely, His love in Holy Communion; that is, His very own Self. (1670)

PRAYER

O great Passion! O deep Wounds! O blood shed in abundance! O God of meekness, O cruel death, have mercy on me.

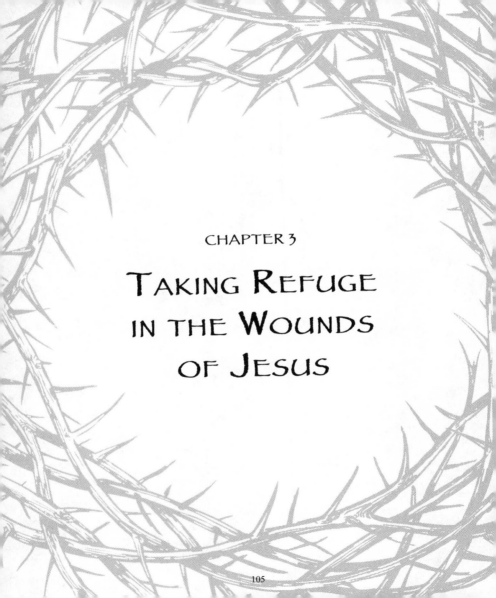

CHAPTER 3

TAKING REFUGE
IN THE WOUNDS
OF JESUS

FAUSTINA: I suffered pain in my body: in my hands, my feet and my side. Jesus is sending me this kind of suffering that I may make reparation for sinners (942). His Passion was imprinted on my body in an invisible manner, but no less painfully (964). In difficult moments I must take refuge in the wounds of Jesus; I must seek consolation, comfort, light, and affirmation in the wounds of Jesus. (226)

INVOCATIONS OF THE PRECIOUS BLOOD OF JESUS BY ST. CATHERINE OF SIENA

St. Catherine of Siena was born in Italy in 1347. She lived, like Jesus, for thirty-three years.

Jesus bestowed on her His sacred wounds and she had a lived experience on how He shed His blood through these wounds. One must remember that Jesus shed His Blood seven times: At the Garden of Gethsemane, at the scourging of the pillar, through His internal wounds, at the carrying of the Cross, in His pierced hands, in His pierced feet, and His pierced heart. This Precious Blood is a path to His mercy and a remedy to heal us.

St. Catherine had a profound devotion to Precious Blood so much that she began her letters with "I write in the Precious Blood of Jesus." She wanted all her words to be cleansed with the Precious Blood. She wrote these powerful invocations of the Precious Blood and prayed them constantly.

Precious Blood, ocean of divine mercy, *flow upon us.*
Precious Blood, most pure offering, *procure us every grace.*

Precious Blood, delight of holy souls, *draw us to You.*
Precious Blood, inexhaustible treasure, *enrich us.*
Precious Blood, furnace of love, *warm our cold hearts.*
Precious Blood, sweet charm of holy souls, *attract us.*
Precious Blood, fount of chastity, *purify us.*
Precious Blood, hope and refuge of sinners, *answer for us.*
Precious Blood, balm of wounded hearts, *console us.*
Precious Blood, efficacious remedy for every suffering, *heal us.*
Precious Blood, refuge of the tempted, *come to our aid.*
Precious Blood, hope of the agonizing, *help us.*
Precious Blood, seed of Christians, *increase our zeal.*
Precious Blood, admiration of the Angels, *exalt us.*
Precious Blood, love of the Seraphim, *enflame us.*
Precious Blood, faith of the Patriarchs, *enlighten us.*
Precious Blood, hope of the Prophets, *strengthen us.*
Precious Blood, charity of the Apostles, *animate us.*
Precious Blood, reward of Confessors, *quicken us.*
Precious Blood, beauty of Virgins, *adorn us.*
Precious Blood, delight of all the Saints, *inebriate us.*
Amen.

PLEADING THE PRECIOUS BLOOD OF JESUS

Father in heaven, may we all be cleansed by the saving Blood of Jesus; may our consciences be purged of dead works. Scripture says that evil is defeated by the Blood of the Lamb, so we ask that the Blood of Jesus cover all who are in need of protection (all civil, religious and lay leaders, our families, friends, enemies, all those for whom we have promised to pray, and ourselves). We mark the borders of our nation and the doorposts of our churches, homes, schools and places of employment with the Precious Blood of Jesus. Also, we cover our vehicles that no one may ever be injured through them. Thank You, Lord, for shedding Your Blood for us. May the Water and Blood that came from the side of Jesus create a protecting fountain of grace, one which flows directly from the throne of God to us. Come, Lord, and fill us with Your Holy Spirit.

ST. THÉRÈSE OF LISIEUX'S
PRAYER TO THE HOLY FACE OF JESUS

Introduction: St. Thérèse of Lisieux was St. Faustina's favorite saint. Writing about the Little Flower, St. Faustina said:

> *I want to write down a dream that I had about Saint Thérèse of the Child Jesus. I was still a novice at the time and was going through some difficulties which I did not know how to overcome. They were interior difficulties connected with exterior ones. I made novenas to various saints, but the situation grew more and more difficult. The sufferings it caused me were so great that I did not know how to go on living, but suddenly the thought occurred to me that I should pray to Saint Thérèse of the Child Jesus. I started a novena to this Saint, because before entering the convent I had had a great devotion to her. Lately, I had somewhat neglected this devotion, but in my need I began again to pray with great fervor.*

> *On the fifth day of the novena, I dreamed of Saint Thérèse,*
> *but it was as if she were still living on earth . . . and began to*
> *comfort me, saying that I should not be worried about this matter,*
> *but should trust more in God. . . . "Sister, know that in three*
> *days the difficulty will come to a happy conclusion." . . . "But,*
> *little Thérèse, shall I be a saint as you are, raised to the altar?"*
> *And she answered, "Yes, you will be a saint just as I am, but*
> *you must trust in the Lord Jesus." (150)*

Modeling St. Faustina, we can pray to the Holy Face:

O Jesus, who in your cruel Passion became the "Reproach of men and the Man of Sorrows," I worship Your Divine Face. Once it shined with the beauty and sweetness of the Divinity. Now for my sake it has become as the face of a "leper." Yet in that disfigured face, I recognize Your infinite love, and I am consumed with the desire of loving You and of making You loved by all mankind. The tears that streamed in such abundance from Your eyes are to me as precious pearls which I delight to gather, that with their infinite worth I may ransom the souls of poor sinners. Amen.

FOR THE SAKE OF YOUR HOLY FACE

My Jesus, to atone for blasphemers I will keep silent when unjustly reprimanded and in this way make partial amends to You. (81)

Eternal Father, I offer Thee the adorable Face of Thy Beloved Son Jesus for the honor and glory of Thy Name, for the conversion of sinners and the salvation of the dying. Amen.

O Jesus, through the merits of your Holy Face, have pity on us, and on the whole world.

(Three times.)

A PRAYER ON CHRIST'S WEARING
A CROWN OF THORNS

FAUSTINA: … I felt a painful thorn in the left side of my head. The suffering continued all day. I meditated continually about how Jesus had been able to endure the pain of so many thorns which made up His crown. I joined my suffering to the suffering of Jesus and offered it for sinners. (349)

Dear Lord, I am grieved when I consider Your sad condition when You wore the Crown of Thorns upon Your holy head. I desire to withdraw the thorns by offering to the Eternal Father the merits of your wounds for the salvation of sinners.

FOR THE SACRED WOUND OF
YOUR PIERCED HEART

JESUS: **From all my wounds, like from streams, mercy flows for souls, but the wound in my Heart is the fountain of unfathomable mercy. From this fountain spring all graces for souls.** (1190)

O my beloved and sweet Jesus, I wish with all the affections of my heart, that all creatures praise, honor, and glorify You eternally for the sacred wound of Your side. I deposit and enclose in the open wound of Your Heart my heart and all my feelings, thoughts, desires, intentions, and all the faculties of my mind. I beg of You, for Your precious Blood and Water that flowed from Your most precious Heart, that You take entire possession of me, that You guide me in all things. Consume me in the burning fire of Your holy Love, so that I may be so absorbed and transformed in You that I am one with You. Amen.

A PRAYER ON THE WOUNDING OF CHRIST'S SHOULDER

FAUSTINA: I saw Jesus in the usual way, and He spoke these words to me: **Lay your head on My shoulder, rest and regain your strength. I am always with you.** (498)

According to tradition, St. Bernard of Clairvaux was told by Jesus that the wound of His left shoulder was more painful than any other. St. Pio of Pietrelcina bore the wounds of Christ and told Fr. Wojtyla (St. John Paul II) that his shoulder wound caused the most pain. The Lord promised to remit venial sins and forget mortal sins to all those who venerated His wound.

St. Thomas Aquinas once noted, quoting St. Gregory, that in meditating on Our Lord's Passion, we could derive strength in knowing there was no trial we could not bear compared to what He suffered.

O lovable Jesus, gentle Lamb of God, I adore You and worship the wound caused by the heavy weight of Your Cross, that burst open Your skin, uncovered the bones of Your Sacred Shoulder and on which Your sorrowing Mother Mary so much sympathized with. I as well, dear Jesus, also sympathize with You, and from the bottom of my heart, I glorify You, and thank You for this painful wound to Your shoulder on which You carried your Cross for my salvation. Ah! for all the sufferings You deeply experienced that increased the enormous weight of Your Cross, I humbly request, have mercy on me, a poor sinful creature, forgive my sins and conduct me to heaven by the way of the Cross.

Holy Mother, imprint in my heart the wounds of the Crucified Jesus Christ.

O Sweet Jesus, please do not be my Judge; be my Savior.

LITANY OF THE SACRED WOUNDS BY ST. CLARE OF ASSISI

JESUS: ... the contemplation of My painful wounds is of great profit to you, and it brings me great joy. (369)

FAUSTINA: As I was praying before the Blessed Sacrament and greeting the five wounds of Jesus, I felt a torrent of graces gushing into my soul giving me a foretaste of heaven and absolute confidence in God's mercy. (1337)

TO THE WOUND IN THE RIGHT HAND

Praise and honor be given You, O my Lord Jesus Christ, by reason of the Sacred Wound in Your Right Hand.

By this adorable wound, I beseech You to pardon me all the sins I have committed by thoughts, words, and deeds, by neglect in Your service, and by self-indulgence, both waking and sleeping. Grant me the grace that, by a devout and frequent remembrance of Your Holy Passion, I may honor Your sacred wounds and the death which You endured for love of me, and that, by chastising my body, I may testify my gratitude for Your sufferings and Your death. Who lives and reigns, world without end. Amen.

Our Father, Hail Mary

TO THE WOUND IN THE LEFT HAND

Praise and honor be given you, O most amiable Jesus, by reason of the Sacred Wound in Your Left Hand.

By this holy wound, I beseech You to have pity on me to change within me whatever is displeasing to You. Grant me to be victorious over my enemies, so that, by the power of Your grace, I may overcome them; and do You, by Your holy and adorable death, deliver me from all dangers, present and to come, and make me worthy to share the glory of Your Blessed Kingdom. Who lives and reigns, world without end. Amen.

Our Father, Hail Mary

TO THE WOUND IN THE RIGHT FOOT

Praise and honor be given You, O sweetest Jesus, by reason of the Sacred Wound in Your Right Foot.

By this holy and adorable wound, I beseech You, to enable me to bring forth worthy fruits of penance for my sins. I humbly entreat You, for the sake of Your adorable death, to keep me, day and night, in Your holy will, to preserve me from all adversity of soul and body, and, on the dreadful day of judgment, to deal with me according to Your mercy, that I may obtain eternal joys. Who lives and reigns, world without end. Amen.

Our Father, Hail Mary

TO THE WOUND OF THE LEFT FOOT

Praise and honor be given You, O sweet Jesus, by reason of the Sacred Wound on Your Left Foot.

By this adorable wound, I beseech You to grant me pardon and full remission of all my sins, so that, with Your aid, I may escape the rigors of justice. I entreat You, O good and merciful Jesus, for the sake of Your holy death, to grant that at the hour of my death, I may have the grace to confess my sins with a perfect contrition, to receive the adorable Sacrament of Your Body and Your Blood, and likewise, the Holy Sacrament of the Sick for my eternal salvation. Who lives and reigns, world without end. Amen.

Our Father, Hail Mary

TO THE WOUND IN THE SACRED SIDE

Praise and honor be given You, O good and sweetest Jesus, by reason of the Wound in Your Sacred Side.

By this adorable wound and by that immense mercy shown Longinus and to us all, in allowing Your Sacred Side to be opened, I beseech You, O good Jesus, that as in Baptism You purified me from original sin, so now You would be pleased, by the merits of Your Most Precious Blood, which is offered up this day over the whole world, to deliver me from all evils, past, present, and to come.

I entreat You, by Your bitter death, to give me a lively faith, a firm hope, and perfect charity, so that I may love You with my whole heart, with my whole soul, and with all my strength. Uphold me by Your grace in the practice of good works, so that I may persevere to the end in Your holy service and glorify You in time and eternity. Amen.

Our Father, Hail Mary

ANIMA CHRISTI

Soul of Christ, sanctify me.
Body of Christ, save me.
Blood of Christ, inebriate me.
Water from the side of Christ, wash me.
Passion of Christ, strengthen me.
O good Jesus, hear me.
Within Thy wounds, hide me.
Never let me be separated from Thee.
From the wicked enemy, defend me.
At the hour of death, call me.
And bid me to come to Thee.
That with Thy saints
I may praise Thee.
Forever and ever. Amen.

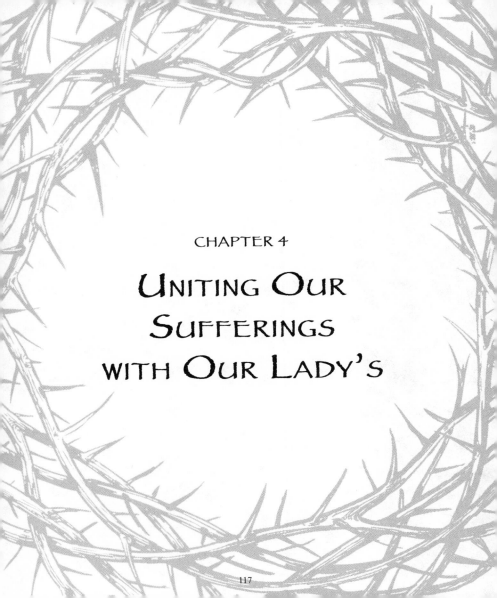

CHAPTER 4

Uniting Our Sufferings with Our Lady's

JESUS: **Pray with all your heart in union with Mary,...** (32)

FAUSTINA: ... I steeped myself in prayer, entrusting myself to the special protection of the Mother of God. She alone is always with me. She, like a good Mother, watches over all my trials and efforts. (798)

Sweet Mother, unite my soul to Jesus, because it is only then that I will be able to endure all trials and tribulations, and only in union with Jesus will my little sacrifices be pleasing to God. Sweetest Mother, continue to teach me about the interior life. May the sword of suffering never break me. O pure Virgin, pour courage into my heart and guard it. (915)

AN ACT OF ABANDONMENT

"Mary, my Mother, do You know how terribly I suffer?" And the Mother of God answered me, *I know how much you suffer, but do not be afraid. I share with you your suffering, and I shall always do so.* (25)

O Jesus, stretched out upon the cross, I implore You, give me the grace of doing faithfully the most holy will of Your Father, in all things, always and everywhere. And when this will of God will seem to me very harsh and difficult to fulfill, it is then I beg You, Jesus, may power and strength flow upon me from Your wounds, and may my lips keep repeating, "Your will be done, O Lord." (1265)

> *Salute Mary, think of Mary, invoke Mary, honor Mary, commend yourselves to Mary, remain with Mary in your house, and walk with Mary when you go out; rejoice with Mary, grieve with Mary, work with Mary, pray with Mary; with Mary carry Jesus in your arms, stand with Mary at the foot of the Cross of Jesus, live and die with Mary and Jesus. Do this and you will live. (Thomas à Kempis)*

REFLECTING ON OUR LADY'S SORROWS: MARY'S SEVEN SWORDS OF PAIN

I heard the voice of Our Lady: *Know, My daughter, that although I was raised to the dignity of Mother of God, seven swords of pain pierced My heart. (786)*

O God, come to my assistance;
O Lord, make haste to help me. Glory be ...

I grieve for you, O Mary most sorrowful, in the affliction of your tender heart at the prophecy of the holy and aged Simeon.

> Dear Mother, by your heart so afflicted, *obtain for me the virtue of humility and the gift of the holy fear of God. Hail Mary.*

I grieve for you, O Mary most sorrowful, in the anguish of your most affectionate heart during the flight into Egypt and your sojourn there.

> Dear Mother, by your heart so troubled, *obtain for me the virtue of generosity, especially toward the poor, and the gift of piety. Hail Mary.*

I grieve for you, O Mary most sorrowful, in those anxieties which tried your troubled heart at the loss of your dear Jesus.

Dear Mother, by your heart so full of anguish, *obtain for me the virtue of chastity and the gift of knowledge. Hail Mary.*

I grieve for you, O Mary most sorrowful, in the consternation of your heart at meeting Jesus as He carried His Cross.

Dear Mother, by your heart so troubled, *obtain for me the virtue of patience and the gift of fortitude. Hail Mary.*

I grieve for you, O Mary most sorrowful, in the martyrdom which your generous heart endured in standing near Jesus in His agony.

Dear Mother, by your afflicted heart, *obtain for me the virtue of temperance and the gift of counsel. Hail Mary.*

I grieve for you, O Mary most sorrowful, in the wounding of your compassionate heart, when the side of Jesus was struck by the lance before His body was removed from the Cross.

Dear Mother, by your heart thus transfixed, *obtain for me the virtue of fraternal charity and the gift of understanding. Hail Mary.*

I grieve for you, O Mary most sorrowful, for the pangs that wrenched your most loving heart at the burial of Jesus.

Dear Mother, by your heart sunk in the bitterness of desolation, *obtain for me the virtue of diligence and the gift of wisdom. Hail Mary.*

Let intercession be made for us, we beg You, O Lord Jesus Christ, now and at the hour of our death, before the throne of Your mercy, by the Blessed Virgin Mary, Your Mother, whose most holy soul was pierced by a sword of sorrow in the hour of Your bitter Passion. Through You, O Jesus

Christ, Savior of the world, who, with the Father and the Holy Spirit, lives and reigns, world without end. Amen.

IMPLORING THE MOTHER OF SORROWS AT THE TIME OF DEATH

O holy Mother, most afflicted by the bitter sorrow which you endured at the foot of the cross during the three hours' agony of Jesus: we implore you, the children of your sorrows, in our last agony, that through your intercession we may pass from the bed of death to form a crown for you in heaven.

Our Father (three times)
Hail Mary (three times)

O Mary, Mother of grace, Mother of mercy,
protect us from the enemy and receive us at the hour of death.
From sudden or unprovided death,
O Lord, deliver us.

From the snares of the devil,
O Lord, deliver us.

From everlasting death,
O Lord, deliver us.

Let us pray. O God, who for the salvation of mankind gave an example and a help in the Passion and Death of your Son: grant, we beseech you, that in the hour of our death, we may experience the effects of this, your charity, and deserve to be partakers in the glory of Him, our Redeemer, through the same Jesus Christ, our Lord. Amen.

Jesus, Mary, and Joseph,
I give you my heart and my soul.

Jesus, Mary, and Joseph,
Assist me in my last agony.

Jesus, Mary, and Joseph,
May I breathe forth my soul in peace with you. Amen.

LITANY OF OUR LADY OF SEVEN SORROWS

Composed by Pope Pius VII while held in captivity by Napoleon

Lord, have mercy on us.
Christ, have mercy on us.
Lord, have mercy on us.
Christ, hear us.
Christ, graciously hear us.

God, the Father of heaven, *have mercy on us.*
God the Son, Redeemer of the world, *have mercy on us.*
God the Holy Spirit, *have mercy on us.*
Holy Trinity, One God, *have mercy on us.*

Holy Mary, Mother of God, *pray for us.*
Holy Virgin of virgins, *pray for us.*
Mother of the Crucified, *pray for us.*
Sorrowful Mother, *pray for us.*
Mournful Mother, *pray for us.*
Sighing Mother, *pray for us.*

Afflicted Mother, *pray for us.*
Forsaken Mother, *pray for us.*
Desolate Mother, *pray for us.*
Mother most sad, *pray for us.*
Mother set around with anguish, *pray for us.*
Mother overwhelmed by grief, *pray for us.*
Mother transfixed by a sword, *pray for us.*
Mother crucified in Thy heart, *pray for us.*
Mother bereaved by Thy Son, *pray for us.*
Sighing Dove, *pray for us.*
Mother of Dolors, *pray for us.*
Fount of tears, *pray for us.*
Sea of bitterness, *pray for us.*
Field of tribulation, *pray for us.*
Mass of suffering, *pray for us.*
Mirror of patience, *pray for us.*
Rock of constancy, *pray for us.*
Remedy of perplexity, *pray for us.*
Joy of the afflicted, *pray for us.*
Ark of the desolate, *pray for us.*
Refuge of the abandoned, *pray for us.*
Shield of the oppressed, *pray for us.*
Conqueror of the incredulous, *pray for us.*
Solace of the wretched, *pray for us.*
Medicine of the sick, *pray for us.*
Help of the faint, *pray for us.*
Strength of the weak, *pray for us.*
Protectress of those who fight, *pray for us.*

Haven of the shipwrecked, *pray for us.*
Calmer of tempests, *pray for us.*
Companion of the sorrowful, *pray for us.*
Retreat of those who groan, *pray for us.*
Terror of the treacherous, *pray for us.*
Standard-bearer of the martyrs, *pray for us.*
Treasure of the faithful, *pray for us.*
Light of confessors, *pray for us.*
Pearl of virgins, *pray for us.*
Comfort of widows, *pray for us.*
Queen of thy servants, *pray for us.*
Joy of all saints, *pray for us.*

Pray for us, most Sorrowful Virgin,
That we may be made worthy of the promises of Christ.

Let us pray.
O God, in whose Passion, according to the prophecy of Simeon, a sword of grief pierced through the most sweet soul of Your glorious Blessed Virgin Mother Mary: grant that we, who celebrate the memory of her Sorrows, may obtain the happy effect of Your Passion, who lives and reigns world without end. Amen.

CONSECRATION TO MARY

O Mary, my sweet Mother,
To you I turn over my soul, my body and my poor heart.
Be the safeguard of my life,
Especially at the hour of death, in the final fight. (161)

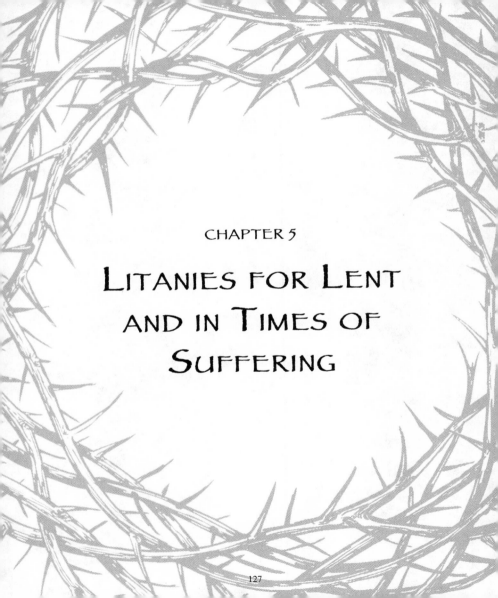

CHAPTER 5

LITANIES FOR LENT AND IN TIMES OF SUFFERING

LITANY OF THE HOLY CROSS

Jesus told Sr. Josefa Menéndez in one of His private revelations to her after His scourging he was "reduced to such a state of pitiful disfigurement as to no longer resemble a human being." After that, His executioners, he told her further, "devoid of every human feeling of humanity, now placed a hard and heavy cross upon my lacerated shoulders."

Litanies are a form of intense prayers imploring God, Our Lord, Our Lady and the saints for aid. They are used as prayers of intercession, peace, pardon, protection, plagues and calamities.

This litany dates from the Middle Ages and from many countries; while the refrain refers to the Holy Cross, it is considered that in doing so, we are actually referring to our Savior Who hung upon it and thereby redeemed us all. By our salutation to the chief instrument of Our Lord's Passion and Death, we trust in hope that He will show mercy to us.

Lord, have mercy.
Lord, have mercy.
Christ, have mercy.
Christ, have mercy.
Lord, have mercy.
Lord, have mercy.
Christ, hear us.
Christ, graciously hear us.

God the Father of heaven, *have mercy on us*.
God the Son, Redeemer of the world, *have mercy on us*.
God the Holy Spirit, our Advocate, *have mercy on us*.
Holy Trinity, one God, *have mercy on us*.

Holy Cross whereon the Lamb of God was offered,
 save us, O Holy Cross.
Hope of Christians, *save us, O Holy Cross*.
Pledge of the resurrection of the dead, *save us, O Holy Cross*.
Shelter of persecuted innocence, *save us, O Holy Cross*.
Guide of the blind, *save us, O Holy Cross*.
Way of those who have gone astray, *save us, O Holy Cross*.
Staff of the lame, *save us, O Holy Cross*.
Consolation of the poor, *save us, O Holy Cross*.
Restraint of the powerful, *save us, O Holy Cross*.
Destruction of the proud, *save us, O Holy Cross*.
Refuge of sinners, *save us, O Holy Cross*.
Trophy of victory over hell, *save us, O Holy Cross*.
Terror of demons, *save us, O Holy Cross*.
Mistress of youth, *save us, O Holy Cross*.
Succor of the distressed, *save us, O Holy Cross*.
Hope of the hopeless, *save us, O Holy Cross*.
Star of the mariner, *save us, O Holy Cross*.
Harbor of the wrecked, *save us, O Holy Cross*.
Rampart of the besieged, *save us, O Holy Cross*.
Father of orphans, *save us, O Holy Cross*.
Defense of widows, *save us, O Holy Cross*.
Counsel of the just, *save us, O Holy Cross*.
Judge of the wicked, *save us, O Holy Cross*.

Rest of the afflicted, *save us, O Holy Cross.*
Safeguard of childhood, *save us, O Holy Cross.*
Strength of manhood, *save us, O Holy Cross.*
Last hope of the aged, *save us, O Holy Cross.*
Light of those who sit in darkness, *save us, O Holy Cross.*
Splendor of kings, *save us, O Holy Cross.*
Civilizer of the world, *save us, O Holy Cross.*
Shield impenetrable, *save us, O Holy Cross.*
Wisdom of the foolish, *save us, O Holy Cross.*
Liberty of slaves, *save us, O Holy Cross.*
Knowledge of the ignorant, *save us, O Holy Cross.*
Sure rule of life, *save us, O Holy Cross.*
Heralded by Prophets, *save us, O Holy Cross.*
Preached by Apostles, *save us, O Holy Cross.*
Glory of Martyrs, *save us, O Holy Cross.*
Study of hermits, *save us, O Holy Cross.*
Chastity of virgins, *save us, O Holy Cross.*
Joy of priests, *save us, O Holy Cross.*
Foundation of the Church, *save us, O Holy Cross.*
Salvation of the world, *save us, O Holy Cross.*
Destruction of idolatry, *save us, O Holy Cross.*
Condemnation of the ungodly, *save us, O Holy Cross.*
Support of the weak, *save us, O Holy Cross.*
Medicine of the sick, *save us, O Holy Cross.*
Health of the leprous, *save us, O Holy Cross.*
Strength of the paralytic, *save us, O Holy Cross.*
Bread of the hungry, *save us, O Holy Cross.*
Fountain of those who thirst, *save us, O Holy Cross.*

Lamb of God, who takes away the sins of the world,
    spare us, O Lord.
Lamb of God, Who takes away the sins of the world,
    hear us, O Lord.
Lamb of God, Who takes away the sins of the world,
    have mercy on us.
Christ, hear us.
Christ, graciously hear us.
Lord, have mercy.
Christ, have mercy.
Lord, have mercy.

We adore You, O Christ, and we praise You,
Because by Your Holy Cross You have redeemed the world.

Behold the Cross of the Lord! Begone, you evil powers!
The Lion of the tribe of Judah, the Root of David, has conquered!
Alleluia!

Let us pray. O God, Who for the redemption of the world, was pleased
to be born in a stable and to die upon a cross; O Lord Jesus Christ, by
Your holy sufferings, which we, Your unworthy servants, call to mind:
by Your Holy Cross, and by Your death, deliver us from the pains of hell,
and promise to conduct us where You conducted the good thief who was
crucified with You, Who lives and reigns eternally in heaven. Amen.

Sweet the wood, sweet the nails,
sweet the Burden which you bore,
for me alone, O Holy Cross,
was worthy to bear the King and Lord of heaven.
Amen.

LITANY OF THE MOST PRECIOUS BLOOD OF JESUS

Lord, have mercy on us.
Christ, have mercy on us.
Lord, have mercy on us.

Christ, hear us.
Christ, graciously hear us.

God, the Father of heaven, *have mercy on us.*
God the Son, Redeemer of the world, *have mercy on us.*
God, the Holy Spirit, *have mercy on us.*
Holy Trinity, One God, *have mercy on us.*

Blood of Christ, only-begotten Son of the Eternal Father, *save us.*
Blood of Christ, Incarnate Word of God, *save us.*
Blood of Christ, of the New and Eternal Testament, *save us.*
Blood of Christ, falling upon the earth in the Agony, *save us.*
Blood of Christ, shed profusely in the Scourging, *save us.*
Blood of Christ, flowing forth in the Crowning with Thorns, *save us.*
Blood of Christ, poured out on the Cross, *save us.*
Blood of Christ, price of our salvation, *save us.*
Blood of Christ, without which there is no forgiveness, *save us.*
Blood of Christ, Eucharistic drink and refreshment of souls, *save us.*
Blood of Christ, stream of mercy, *save us.*
Blood of Christ, victor over demons, *save us.*
Blood of Christ, courage of martyrs, *save us.*
Blood of Christ, strength of confessors, *save us.*
Blood of Christ, bringing forth virgins, *save us.*

Blood of Christ, help of those in peril, *save us.*
Blood of Christ, relief of the burdened, *save us.*
Blood of Christ, solace in sorrow, *save us.*
Blood of Christ, hope of the penitent, *save us.*
Blood of Christ, consolation of the dying, *save us.*
Blood of Christ, peace and tenderness of hearts, *save us.*
Blood of Christ, pledge of eternal life, *save us.*
Blood of Christ, freeing souls from purgatory, *save us.*
Blood of Christ, most worthy of all glory and honor, *save us.*

Lamb of God, who takes away the sins of the world,
   spare us, O Lord.
Lamb of God, who takes away the sins of the world,
   graciously hear us, O Lord.
Lamb of God, who takes away the sins of the world,
   have mercy on us.

You have redeemed us, O Lord, in Your Blood.
And made us, for our God, a kingdom.

Let us pray. Almighty and eternal God, You have appointed Your only-begotten Son the Redeemer of the world and willed to be appeased by His blood. Grant, we beg You, that we may worthily adore this price of our salvation and through its power be safeguarded from the evils of the present life so that we may rejoice in its fruits forever in heaven. Through the same Christ our Lord. Amen.

A LITANY IN TIMES OF SUFFERING

Based on the words of St. Faustina

When my day seems overflowing with little crosses, *be with me Lord.*
When I'm dealing with poor health and my strength is fading,
   be with me Lord.
When even the smallest acts of self-denial seem impossible,
   be with me Lord.
When others treat me harshly or humiliate me, *be with me Lord.*
When those around me act as if I don't even exist, *be with me Lord.*
When my plans fall apart, *be with me Lord.*
When I'm suffering inside, *be with me Lord.*
When my spirit is dry and barren, *be with me Lord.*
When fear and uncertainty overwhelm me, *be with me Lord.*
When darkness fills me, *be with me Lord.*
When temptations crowd around me, *be with me Lord.*
When indescribable torments cloud my mind and my heart,
   be with me Lord.
When I find it hard to stop complaining or at least to complain less,
   be with me Lord.
When the hour of my death arrives, *be with me Lord.*

Let us pray, for ourselves and for others who are suffering:

Lord of All Comfort, sooth us on difficult and stormy days,
   on days of testing and days of ordeal.

Lord of All Strength, support us when suffering and fatigue
   weigh heavily on our bodies and our souls.

Lord of All Courage, fill us with faith and fortitude
    when we feel so lost and so weak.

Your Divine Mercy brings comfort,

Your Divine Mercy brings strength,

Your Divine Mercy brings courage.

Jesus, I trust in You.

Be with me, Lord.

Amen.

A LITANY OF LONGING

Lord, have mercy on us.
Christ, have mercy on us.
Lord, have mercy on us.
Christ hear us.

Christ, graciously hear us.
God the Father, Creator of the world, *have mercy on us.*
God the Son, Redeemer of the world, *have mercy on us.*
God the Holy Spirit, Truth in the world, *have mercy on us.*
Most Blessed Trinity, One God, *have mercy on us.*

Holy Mary, Mother of God, *pray for us.*
Holy Mary, Queen of all angels, *pray for us.*
Holy Mary, Queen of all saints, *pray for us.*
Holy Mary, Queen of all hearts, *pray for us.*

All you angels and saints, *pray for us.*

Struggling souls full of longing, *we pray for you.*
Abandoned children full of longing, *we pray for you.*
Abandoned youths full of longing, *we pray for you.*
Abandoned mothers, *we pray for you.*
Abandoned sick, *we pray for you.*
Abandoned old and poor, *we pray for you.*
Abandoned homeless, *we pray for you.*
Abandoned ones in danger, *we pray for you.*
Abandoned, straying souls, *we pray for you.*

Abandoned fallen souls, *we pray for you.*
Abandoned desperate souls, *we pray for you.*
Abandoned dying souls, *we pray for you.*

In our painful longing for You, *help us, merciful God.*
In our painful longing for love, *help us, merciful God.*
In our painful longing for understanding, *help us, merciful God.*
In our painful longing for peace, *help us, merciful God.*
In our painful longing for health, *help us, merciful God.*
In our painful longing for our home, *help us, merciful God.*
In our painful longing for tranquility of heart, *help us, merciful God.*
In our painful longing for the forgiveness of our sins,
    help us, merciful God.
In our painful longing to make reparation, *help us, merciful God.*

Promise to quench our longing, loving Father in heaven.
Promise to accept our longing as a sacrifice, Crucified Redeemer.
Promise to sanctify our longing, Comforter, Holy Spirit.

Take us firmly by the hand, O holy angels, and do not
   let any of us be lost.

Place us under your protective mantle, Blessed Mary, Mother of Grace.

Holy God, Holy Mighty One, Holy Immortal One, lead us home to
You, where all our longing will be eternally fulfilled, healed, and transformed into joy. Amen.

A LITANY OF FASTING

JESUS: ... the smallest sacrifice finds great value in My eyes, ... (639)

St. Faustina fasted exhaustively. It's one of the best ways to love God
and our neighbor, and it helps us say no to temptation by inviting the
Holy Spirit into our hearts. If we are more virtuous, we will naturally
be kinder to our neighbor.

Help me fast from fear, and feast on trust. *Jesus, I trust in You.*
Help me fast from pressure, and feast on prayer. *Jesus, I trust in You.*
Help me fast from self-concern, and feast on compassion for others.
   Jesus, I trust in You.
Help me fast from discouragement, and feast on hope.
   Jesus, I trust in You.
Help me fast from discontent, and feast on gratitude.
   Jesus, I trust in You.
Help me fast from judging others, and feast on Christ dwelling in them.
   Jesus, I trust in You.
Help me fast from words that destroy and feast on words that build.
   Jesus, I trust in You.

Help me fast from idle gossip, and feast on silence. *Jesus, I trust in You.*
Help me fast from anger, and feast on patience. *Jesus, I trust in You.*
Help me fast from ill thoughts, and feast on the healing power of God.
Jesus, I trust in You.
Help me fast from bitterness, and feast on forgiveness.
Jesus, I trust in You.
Help me fast from the shadows of sorrow, and feast on
the light of the Resurrection. *Jesus, I trust in You.*

Lord, have mercy.
Christ, have mercy.
Lord, have mercy.

Let us pray. I thank You, Heavenly Father, for giving me the grace to fast. Grant that I may discover Your immeasurable love with which You love all creatures. Fill us with the Spirit of prayer and fasting so we may recognize and fulfill Your will; to love You above everything else and to love our neighbors as ourselves. Amen.

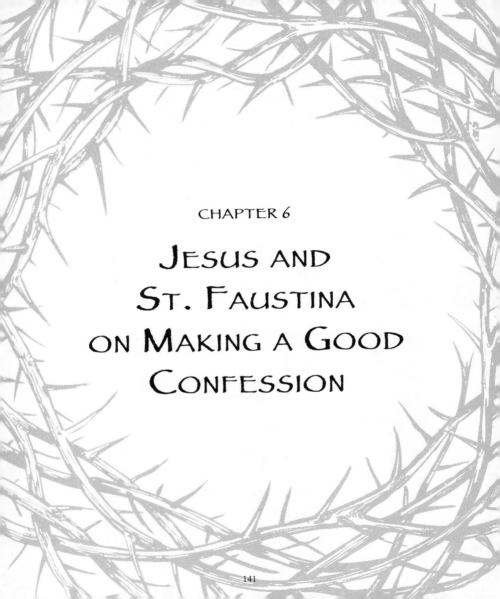

CHAPTER 6

Jesus and St. Faustina on Making a Good Confession

JESUS: **Do not put off the Sacrament of Penance, because this displeases Me.** (1464)

FAUSTINA: Oh, may God keep every soul from delaying confession until the last hour! I understood the great power of the priest's words when they are poured out upon the sick person's soul. (321)

JESUS: **You are dealing with the God of mercy, which your misery cannot exhaust. Remember, I did not allot only a certain number of pardons.** (1488)

JESUS SPEAKS:

First, do not fight against a temptation by yourself, but disclose it to the confessor at once, and then the temptation will lose all its force. (1560)

... it suffices to come with faith to the feet of my representative and to reveal to him one's misery and the miracle of Divine Mercy will be fully demonstrated. (1448)

Be absolutely as frank as possible with your confessor. (1499)

Daughter, when you go to confession, to this fountain of My mercy, the Blood and Water which came forth from My Heart always flows down upon your soul and ennobles it. Every time you go to confession, immerse yourself entirely in My mercy, with great trust, so that I may pour the bounty of My grace upon your soul. (1602).

My daughter, just as you prepare in My presence, so also you make your confession before Me. The person of the priest is, for Me, only a screen. Never analyze what sort of a priest it is that I am making

use of; open your soul in confession as you would to Me, and I will fill it with My light. (1725)

FAUSTINA SPEAKS:

Concerning Holy Confession. We should derive two kinds of profit from Holy Confession:

1. We come to confession to be healed;
2. We come to be educated—like a small child, our soul has constant need of education. (377)

I shall pay special attention to two things: firstly, I will choose, in making my confession, that which humiliates me most, even if it be a trifle, but something that costs me much, and for that reason I will tell it; secondly, I will practice contrition, not only during confession, but during every self-examination, and I will arouse within myself an act of perfect contrition, especially when I am going to bed. (377)

… I would like to say three words to the soul that is determined to strive for sanctity and to derive fruit; that is to say, benefit from confession.

First [word]—complete sincerity and openness.
Second word—humility.
Third word—obedience. (113)

A strong temptation. The Lord gave me to know how pleasing a pure heart is to Him, and thereby I was given a deeper knowledge of my own misery. When I began to prepare for confession, strong temptations against confessors assaulted me. I did not see Satan, but I could sense him, his terrible anger.—"Yes, he's an ordinary man."—"Not ordinary, because he has the power of God."—Yes, it is not difficult for me to accuse myself of my sins. But to uncover the most secret depths of my heart, to give an account of the action of God's grace, to speak about God's every demand, about all that goes on between God and myself.... To tell that to a man is beyond my strength. I felt I was fighting against the powers and I cried out: "O Christ, You and the priest are one; I will approach confession as if I were approaching, not a man, but You." When I entered the confessional, I began by disclosing my difficulties. The priest replied that the best thing I could have done was to disclose these temptations from the outset. However, after the confession, they took flight, and my soul is enjoying peace. (1715)

As regards Holy Confession, I shall choose what costs and humiliates me most. Sometimes a trifle costs more than something greater. I will call to mind the Passion of Jesus at each confession, to arouse my heart to contrition. Insofar as possible, with the grace of God, I will always practice perfect contrition. I will devote more time to this contrition. Before I approach the confessional, I shall first enter the open and most merciful Heart of the Savior. When I leave the confessional, I shall rouse in my soul great gratitude to the Holy Trinity for this wonderful and inconceivable miracle of mercy that is wrought in my soul. And the more miserable my soul is, the more I feel the ocean of God's mercy engulfing me and giving me strength and great power. (225)

When I went to confession, I did not even know how to confess. However, the priest [probably Father Casimir Ratkiewicz] recognized the condition of my soul at once and said to me, "Despite everything, you are on the way to salvation; you are on the right path, but God may leave your soul in this darkness and obscurity until death, and the former light may never return. But in all things abandon yourself to the will of God." (1205)

One thing alone is necessary; that the sinner set ajar the door of his heart, be it ever so little, to let in a ray of God's merciful grace, and then God will do the rest. (1507)

DIRECTIVES FROM FAUSTINA'S CONFESSORS

Toward the end of my novitiate, a confessor [perhaps Father Theodore] told me: "Go through life doing good, so that I could write on its pages: "She spent her life doing good." May God bring this about in you."

Another time the confessor said to me, "Comport yourself before God like the widow in the Gospel; although the coin she dropped into the box was of little value, it counted far more before God than all the big offerings of others."

On another occasion the instruction I received was this: "Act in such a way that all those who come in contact with you will go away joyful. Sow happiness about you because you have received much from God; give then generously to others. They should take leave of you with their hearts filled with joy, even if they have no more than touched the hem of your garment. Keep well in mind the words I am telling you right now." (55)

APPENDICES

APPENDIX A
THE DIVINE MERCY PROMISES

Throughout her *Diary*, St. Faustina recorded promises Jesus made *not only to her but to those who would pray to, promote, and trust in Divine Mercy.*

TO THOSE SOULS WHO VENERATE THE IMAGE OF DIVINE MERCY

I promise that the soul that will venerate this image will not perish. I also promise victory over [its] enemies already here on earth, especially at the hour of death. I Myself will defend it as My own glory. (48)

TO THOSE SOULS WHO PRAY THE CHAPLET OF DIVINE MERCY

The souls that say this chaplet will be embraced by My mercy during their lifetime and especially at the hour of their death. (754)

When hardened sinners say it, I will fill their souls with peace, and the hour of their death will be a happy one. (1541)

... [W]hen they say this chaplet in the presence of the dying, I will stand between My Father and the dying person, not as the just Judge but as the merciful Savior. (1541)

Whoever will recite it will receive great mercy at the hour of death.... Even if there were a sinner most hardened, if he were to recite this chaplet only once, he would receive grace from My infinite mercy. (687)

TO THOSE SOULS WHO HONOR AND SPREAD THE WORSHIP OF DIVINE MERCY

I Myself will defend as My own glory, during their lifetime, and especially at the hour of their death, those souls who will venerate My fathomless mercy. (1225)

... All those souls who will glorify My mercy and spread its worship, encouraging others to trust in My mercy, will not experience terror at the hour of death. My mercy will shield them in that final battle.... (1540)

Souls who spread the honor of My mercy I shield through their entire lives as a tender mother her infant, and at the hour of death I will not be a Judge for them, but the merciful Savior.... Happy is the soul that during its lifetime immersed itself in the Fountain of Mercy, because justice will have no hold on it. (1075)

TO THOSE SOULS WHO PUT THEIR TRUST IN DIVINE MERCY

He who trusts in My mercy will not perish, for all his affairs are Mine, and his enemies will be shattered at the base of My footstool. (723)

Souls that make an appeal to My mercy delight Me. To such souls I grant even more graces than they ask. (1146)

Every soul believing and trusting in My mercy will obtain it. (420)

TO THOSE SOULS WHO HONOR THE HOUR OF MERCY

This is the hour of great mercy for the whole world. I will allow you to enter into My mortal sorrow. In this hour, I will refuse nothing to the soul that makes a request of Me in virtue of My Passion.... (1320)

TO PRIESTS WHO PROCLAIM AND EXTOL THE DIVINE MERCY

To priests who proclaim and extol My mercy, I will give wondrous power; I will anoint their words and touch the hearts of those to whom they will speak. (1521)

OUR LORD'S PROMISES ATTACHED TO THE PRAYING OF THE CHAPLET OF DIVINE MERCY AS REVEALED TO ST. FAUSTINA

In addition to verses shared with the Divine Mercy Promises (48, 754, 1541, 687, 1521, and 1387), the Promises Attached to the Praying of the Chaplet also include:

At three o'clock, implore My mercy, especially for sinners; and, if only for a brief moment, immerse yourself in My Passion, particularly in My abandonment at the moment of agony. This is the hour of great mercy for the whole world. I will allow you to enter into My mortal sorrow. In this hour, I will refuse nothing to the soul that makes a request of me in virtue of My Passion.... (1320; also cf. 1572)

Souls who spread the honor of My mercy ... at the hour of death I will not be a Judge for them, but the Merciful Savior. (1075)

The two rays denote Blood and Water.... These two rays issued from the very depths of My tender mercy when My agonized Heart was opened by a lance on the Cross. These rays shield souls from the wrath of My Father.... I desire that the first Sunday after Easter be the Feast of Mercy.... [W]hoever approaches the Fount of Life on this day will be granted complete remission of sins and punishment. Mankind will not have peace until it turns with trust to My mercy. (299–300)

I desire that the Feast of Mercy be a refuge and shelter for all souls.... The soul that will go to Confession and receive Holy Communion shall obtain complete forgiveness of sins and punishment.... It is My desire that [the Feast] be solemnly celebrated on the first Sunday after Easter.... (699)

Through the chaplet you will obtain everything, if what you ask for is compatible with My will. (1731)

My mercy is greater than your sins and those of the entire world. (1485)

THE CHAPLET OF DIVINE MERCY — FOR THE SAKE OF HIS SORROWFUL PASSION

JESUS: **Say unceasingly the chaplet that I have taught you. Whoever will recite it will receive great mercy at the hour of death.** (687)

Traditionally, a five-decade rosary is used for praying the Divine Mercy Chaplet.

1. Begin with the Sign of the Cross, one Our Father, one Hail Mary, and the Apostles' Creed.

2. On the Our Father bead pray:

    Eternal Father, I offer You the Body and Blood, Soul and Divinity of Your dearly beloved Son, Our Lord Jesus Christ, in atonement for our sins and those of the whole world.

3. On the ten Hail Mary beads pray:

For the sake of His sorrowful Passion, have mercy on us and on the whole world.

(Repeat steps 2 and 3 for all five decades.)

4. After the fifth decade, conclude the chaplet by praying three times:

Holy God, Holy Mighty One, Holy Immortal One, have mercy on us and on the whole world.

APPENDIX C

PROMISES OF THE CHAPLET FOR SPECIAL GRACES

St. Faustina lamented to Jesus how greatly concerned she was for all mankind. He told her to say the chaplet to bring humankind closer to Him. Here are ways you can pray the chaplet for various needs. Pray it unceasingly.

FOR THOSE WHO ARE DEVOTED TO THE CHAPLET

The souls that say this chaplet will be embraced by My mercy during their lifetime and especially at the hour of their death. (754)

While I was saying the chaplet, I heard a voice which said, **Oh, what great graces I will grant to souls who say this chaplet; the very depths of My tender mercy are stirred for the sake of those who say the chaplet.** O what a great multitude of souls I see! They worshipped the

Divine Mercy and will be singing the hymn of praise for all eternity. (848)

TO APPEASE HIS ANGER

This prayer will serve to appease My wrath. (476)

When this chaplet is said by the bedside of a dying person, God's anger is placated, ... (811)

This chaplet mitigates God's anger, as He Himself told me. (1036)

It [the chaplet] appeases the anger of God. (1565)

FOR THE DYING

At the hour of their death, I defend as My own glory every soul that will say this chaplet; or when others say it for a dying person, the pardon is the same. When this chaplet is said by the bedside of a dying person, God's anger is placated, unfathomable mercy envelops the soul, and the very depths of My tender mercy are moved for the sake of the sorrowful Passion of My Son. (811)

I realize more and more how much every soul needs God's mercy throughout life and particularly at the hour of death. This chaplet mitigates God's anger, as He Himself told me. (1036)

Pray as much as you can for the dying. By your entreaties, obtain for them trust in My mercy, because they have most need of trust, and have it the least. Be assured that the grace of eternal salvation for certain souls in their final moment depends on your prayer. (1777)

DYING IN PEACE

The sick man peacefully breathed his last. When I came to myself, I understood how very important the chaplet was for the dying. It appeases the anger of God. (1565)

FOR THE CONVERSION OF SINNERS

Priests will recommend it to sinners as their last hope of salvation. Even if there were a sinner most hardened, if he were to recite this chaplet only once, he would receive grace from My infinite mercy. (687)

When hardened sinners say it, I will fill their souls with peace, and the hour of their death will be a happy one. (1541)

FOR SOULS IN DESPAIR

Today, the Lord came to me and said, **My daughter, help Me to save souls. You will go to a dying sinner, and you will continue to recite the chaplet, and in this way you will obtain for him trust in My mercy, for he is already in despair.** (1797)

Suddenly, I found myself in a strange cottage where an elderly man was dying amidst great torments. All about the bed was a multitude of demons and the family, who were crying. When I began to pray, the spirits of darkness fled, with hissing and threats directed at me. The soul became calm and, filled with trust, rested in the Lord. At the same moment, I found myself again in my own room. How this happens ... I do not know. (1798)

DEMONS FLEE IN PANIC

When I entered the chapel for a moment, the Lord said to me, **My daughter, help Me to save a certain dying sinner. Say the chaplet that I have taught you for him.** When I began to say the chaplet, I saw the man dying in the midst of terrible torment and struggle. His Guardian Angel was defending him, but he was, as it were, powerless against the enormity of the soul's misery. A multitude of devils was waiting for the soul. But while I was saying the chaplet, I saw Jesus just as He is depicted in the image. The rays which issued from Jesus' Heart enveloped the sick man, and the powers of darkness fled in panic. The sick man peacefully breathed his last. (1565)

AGAINST STORMS

Today I was awakened by a great storm. The wind was raging, and it was raining in torrents, thunderbolts striking again and again. I began to pray that the storm would do no harm, when I heard the words: **Say the chaplet I have taught you, and the storm will cease.** I began immediately to say the chaplet and hadn't even finished it when the storm suddenly ceased, and I heard the words: **Through the chaplet you will obtain everything, if what you ask for is compatible with My will.** (1731)

When a great storm was approaching, I began to say the chaplet. Suddenly I heard the voice of an angel: "I cannot approach in this storm, because the light which comes from her mouth drives back both me and the storm." Such was the angel's complaint to God. I then recognized how much havoc he was to have made through this storm; but I also recognized that this prayer was pleasing to God, and that this chaplet was most powerful. (1791)

A NOVENA TO THE DIVINE MERCY FOR THE CONVERSION OF THE WORLD

On Good Friday, 1937, Jesus requested that St. Faustina make a special novena. "I am to begin it for the conversion of the whole world and for the recognition of The Divine Mercy...."

> JESUS: **So that every soul will praise My goodness. I desire trust from My creatures. Encourage souls to place great trust in My fathomless mercy. Let the weak, sinful soul have no fear to approach Me, for even if it had more sins than there are grains of sand in the world, all would be drowned in the unmeasurable depths of My mercy. (1059)**

The Lord dictated the intentions for each day. Faustina was to bring to His Heart a different group of souls each day and immerse them in the ocean of His mercy.

JESUS: **I desire that during these nine days you bring souls to the fountain of My mercy, that they may draw therefrom strength and refreshment and whatever grace they need in the hard- ships of life, and especially at the hour of death.** (1209)

FIRST DAY

Today, bring to Me all mankind, especially all sinners,... (1210)

Most Merciful Jesus, whose very nature it is to have compassion on us and to forgive us, do not look upon our sins but upon our trust which we place in Your infinite goodness. Receive us all into the abode of Your Most Compassionate Heart, and never let us escape from it. We beg this of You by Your love which unites You to the Father and the Holy Spirit....

Eternal Father, turn Your merciful gaze upon all mankind and especially upon poor sinners, all enfolded in the Most Compassionate Heart of Jesus. For the sake of His sorrowful Passion, show us Your mercy, that we may praise the omnipotence of Your mercy forever and ever. Amen. (1211)

SECOND DAY

Today bring to Me the souls of priests and religious. (1212)

Most merciful Jesus, from whom comes all that is good, increase Your grace in us, that we may perform worthy works of mercy, and that all who see them may glorify the Father of Mercy who is in heaven....

Eternal Father, turn your merciful gaze upon the company [of chosen ones] in Your vineyard—upon the souls of priests and religious; and endow them with the strength of Your blessing. For the love of the Heart of Your Son in which they are enfolded, impart to them Your power and light, that they may be able to guide others in the way of salvation, and with one voice sing praise to Your boundless mercy for ages without end. Amen. (1213)

THIRD DAY

Today bring to Me all devout and faithful souls. (1214)

Most Merciful Jesus, from the treasury of Your mercy You impart Your graces in great abundance to each and all. Receive us into the abode of Your Most Compassionate Heart and never let us escape from It. We beg this of You by that most wondrous love for the heavenly Father with which Your Heart burns so fiercely....

Eternal Father, turn Your merciful gaze upon faithful souls, as upon the inheritance of Your Son. For the sake of His sorrowful Passion, grant them Your blessing and surround them with Your constant protection. Thus may they never fail in love or lose the treasure of the holy faith, but rather, with all the hosts of Angels and Saints, may they glorify Your boundless mercy for endless ages. Amen. (1215)

FOURTH DAY

Today bring to Me the pagans and those who do not yet know Me. (1216)

Most Compassionate Jesus, You are the Light of the whole world. Receive into the abode of Your Most Compassionate Heart the souls of pagans who as yet do not know You. Let the rays of Your grace enlighten them that they, too, together with us, may extol Your wonderful mercy; and do not let them escape from the abode which is Your Most Compassionate Heart....

Eternal Father, turn Your merciful gaze upon the souls of pagans and of those who as yet do not know You, but who are enclosed in the Most Compassionate Heart of Jesus. Draw them to the light of the Gospel. These souls do not know what great happiness it is to love You. Grant that they, too, may extol the generosity of Your mercy for endless ages. Amen. (1217)

FIFTH DAY

Today bring to Me the souls of the heretics and schismatics, ... (1218)

Most Merciful Jesus, Goodness Itself, You do not refuse light to those who seek it of You. Receive into the abode of Your Most Compassionate Heart the souls of heretics and schismatics. Draw them by Your light into the unity of the Church, and do not let them escape from the abode of Your Most Compassionate Heart; but bring it about that they, too, come to extol the generosity of Your mercy....

Eternal Father, turn Your merciful gaze upon the souls of heretics and schismatics, who have squandered Your blessings and misused Your graces by obstinately persisting in their errors. Do not look upon their errors, but upon the love of Your own Son and upon His bitter Passion, which He underwent for their sake, since they, too, are enclosed in the Most

Compassionate Heart of Jesus. Bring it about that they also may glorify Your great mercy for endless ages. Amen. (1219)

SIXTH DAY

Today bring to Me the meek and humble souls and the souls of little children,... (1220)

Most Merciful Jesus, You Yourself have said, "Learn from Me for I am meek and humble of heart." Receive into the abode of Your Most Compassionate Heart all meek and humble souls and the souls of little children. These souls send all heaven into ecstasy and they are the heavenly Father's favorites. They are a sweet-smelling bouquet before the throne of God; God Himself takes delight in their fragrance. These souls have a permanent abode in Your Most Compassionate Heart, O Jesus, and they unceasingly sing out a hymn of love and mercy.... (1221)

Eternal Father, turn Your merciful gaze upon meek souls and humble souls, and upon the souls of little children who are enfolded in the abode which is the Most Compassionate Heart of Jesus. These souls bear the closest resemblance to Your Son. Their fragrance rises from the earth and reaches Your very throne. Father of mercy and of all goodness, I beg You by the love You bear these souls and by the delight You take in them: Bless the whole world, that all souls together may sing out the praises of Your mercy for endless ages. Amen. (1223)

SEVENTH DAY

Today bring to Me the souls who especially venerate and glorify My mercy, ... (1224)

Most Merciful Jesus, whose Heart is Love Itself, receive into the abode of Your Most Compassionate Heart the souls of those who particularly extol and venerate the greatness of Your mercy. These souls are mighty with the very power of God Himself. In the midst of all afflictions and adversities they go forward, confident of Your mercy. These souls are united to Jesus and carry all mankind on their shoulders. These souls will not be judged severely, but Your mercy will embrace them as they depart from this life....

Eternal Father, turn Your merciful gaze upon the souls who glorify and venerate Your greatest attribute, that of Your fathomless mercy, and who are enclosed in the Most Compassionate Heart of Jesus. These souls are a living Gospel; their hands are full of deeds of mercy, and their spirit, overflowing with joy, sings a canticle of mercy to You, O Most High! I beg You, O God: Show them Your mercy according to the hope and trust they have placed in You. Let there be accomplished in them the promise of Jesus, who said to them, **I Myself will defend as My own glory, during their lifetime, and especially at the hour of their death, those souls who will venerate My fathomless mercy.** (1225)

EIGHTH DAY

Today bring to Me the souls who are in the prison of Purgatory, ... (1226)

Most Merciful Jesus, Your Yourself have said that You desire mercy; so I bring into the abode of Your Most Compassionate Heart the souls in Purgatory, souls who are very dear to You, and yet, who must make retribution to Your justice. May the streams of Blood and Water which gushed forth from Your Heart put out the flames of purifying fire, that in that place, too, the power of Your mercy may be praised....

Eternal Father, turn Your merciful gaze upon the souls suffering in Purgatory, who are enfolded in the Most Compassionate Heart of Jesus. I beg You, by the sorrowful Passion of Jesus Your Son, and by all the bitterness with which His most sacred Soul was flooded, manifest Your mercy to the souls who are under Your just scrutiny. Look upon them in no other way than through the Wounds of Jesus, Your dearly beloved Son; for we firmly believe that there is no limit to Your goodness and compassion. (1227)

NINTH DAY

Today bring to Me souls who have become lukewarm,... (1228)

Most compassionate Jesus, You are Compassion Itself. I bring lukewarm souls into the abode of Your Most Compassionate Heart. In this fire of Your pure love let these tepid souls, who, like corpses, filled You with such deep loathing, be once again set aflame. O Most Compassionate Jesus, exercise the omnipotence of Your mercy and draw them into the very ardor of Your love; and bestow upon them the gift of holy love, for nothing is beyond Your power....

Eternal Father, turn Your merciful gaze upon lukewarm souls, who are nonetheless enfolded in the Most Compassionate Heart of Jesus. Father of Mercy, I beg You by the bitter Passion of Your Son and by His three-hour agony on the Cross: Let them, too, glorify the abyss of Your mercy. (1229)

APPENDIX E

INDULGENCES

What is an indulgence?

"An indulgence is a remission before God of the temporal punishment due to sins whose guilt has already been forgiven, which the faithful Christian who is duly disposed gains under certain prescribed conditions through the action of the Church which, as the minister of redemption, dispenses and applies with authority the treasury of the satisfactions of Christ and the saints."

"An indulgence is partial or plenary according as it removes either part or all of the temporal punishment due to sin." The faithful can gain indulgences for themselves or apply them to the dead. (CCC 1471)

An indulgence is granted to the Christian faithful who devoutly visit a cemetery and pray, if only silently, for the dead. This indulgence is applicable only to the souls in purgatory. This indulgence is a plenary one, from November 1 through November 8. On other days of the year, it is a partial indulgence.

This indulgence also calls for:

- Reception of sacramental confession.
- Reception of Holy Communion.
- Performance of the prescribed work, such as Stations of the Cross, the Rosary, etc.
- Praying for the pope's intentions—for example, the Our Father, Hail Mary, or any pious prayer.
- That all conditions are met within eight days prior to or after the prescribed work.

WHAT ARE OTHER DEVOTIONS THAT GRANT INDULGENCES?

- Nine First Fridays: For the practice of the Nine First Fridays devotion, Our Lord promises the grace of final repentance.
- Five First Saturdays: For the practice of the Five First Saturdays devotion, Our Lady promises to assist at the hour of death with the graces necessary for salvation.

BIBLIOGRAPHY

Kosicki, George, W., C.S.B. *Revelations of Divine Mercy: Daily Readings from the Diary of Blessed Faustina Kowalska.* Ann Arbor, MI: Servant Publications, 1996.

———. *Mercy Minutes.* Stockbridge, MA: Marian Press, 2016.

———. *Divine Mercy Minutes with Jesus.* Stockbridge, MA: Marian Press, 2008.

Kowalska, St. Maria Faustina. *Divine Mercy in My Soul: Diary of Saint Maria Faustina Kowalska.* Stockbridge, MA: Marian Press, 1987.

Order of Canons Regular of the Holy Cross, Carrollton, OH: *Litany of Longing.* Used with permission.

RESOURCES

For information about the National Shrine of The Divine Mercy and to become a Friend of Mercy, go to www.thedivinemercy.org.

Association of Marian Helpers
Eden Hill, Stockbridge, MA 01263

Holy Souls Sodality
c/o Association of Marian Helpers
Eden Hill, Stockbridge, MA 01263
www.prayforsouls.org

For memberships and to obtain Masses and Gregorian Masses:

Pious Union of St. Joseph
953 East Michigan Avenue, Grass Lake, MI 49249
(517) 522-8017
www.pusj.org

ABOUT THE AUTHOR

Susan Tassone has long been a passionate champion for the holy souls in purgatory and is recognized as leading a worldwide "purgatory movement." The award-winning author of thirteen best sellers, including *Jesus Speaks to Faustina and You, Day by Day with Saint Faustina, St. Faustina Prayer Book for Adoration, St. Faustina Prayer Book for the Conversion of Sinners, St. Faustina Prayer Book for the Holy Souls in Purgatory,* and *Day by Day for the Holy Souls in Purgatory.* Susan shares her passion for saving souls through innumerable speaking engagements throughout the country. More than a dozen cardinals and bishops around the world have endorsed her works.

She is a frequent, popular guest on national radio and television programs, as well as having a major impact through social media. EWTN Global Catholic Network declared that Susan is the all-time best-selling author in the history of EWTN. In 2017, she appeared on the cover of

Catholic Digest. In 2013, she was featured in the groundbreaking documentary *Purgatory: The Forgotten Church*, bringing her unique style and penetrating message to a new generation.

Through her tireless work, she raises awareness of purgatory as well as donations for Masses for the holy souls.

Susan holds a master's degree in religious education from Loyola University Chicago, and in addition to her numerous awards, she has had the privilege and honor of being granted two private audiences with St. John Paul II, who bestowed a special blessing on her ministry for the holy souls.

Learn more at: susantassone.com.

Sophia Institute

Sophia Institute is a nonprofit institution that seeks to nurture the spiritual, moral, and cultural life of souls and to spread the Gospel of Christ in conformity with the authentic teachings of the Roman Catholic Church.

Sophia Institute Press fulfills this mission by offering translations, reprints, and new publications that afford readers a rich source of the enduring wisdom of mankind.

Sophia Institute also operates the popular online resource CatholicExchange.com. *Catholic Exchange* provides world news from a Catholic perspective as well as daily devotionals and articles that will help readers to grow in holiness and live a life consistent with the teachings of the Church.

In 2013, Sophia Institute launched Sophia Institute for Teachers to renew and rebuild Catholic culture through service to Catholic education. With the goal of nurturing the spiritual, moral, and cultural life of souls, and an abiding respect for the role and work of teachers, we strive to provide materials and programs that are at once enlightening to the mind and ennobling to the heart; faithful and complete, as well as useful and practical.

Sophia Institute gratefully recognizes the Solidarity Association for preserving and encouraging the growth of our apostolate over the course of many years. Without their generous and timely support, this book would not be in your hands.

www.SophiaInstitute.com
www.CatholicExchange.com
www.SophiaInstituteforTeachers.org

Sophia Institute Press® is a registered trademark of Sophia Institute.
Sophia Institute is a tax-exempt institution as defined by the
Internal Revenue Code, Section 501(c)(3). Tax ID 22-2548708.